God's Grace in the Midst of the Storms

A Family Journey in the World of Schizophrenia

Barbara A. Covington

authorHOUSE®

AuthorHouse™
1663 Liberty Drive
Bloomington, IN 47403
www.authorhouse.com
Phone: 1-800-839-8640

First published by AuthorHouse   5/2/2011

ISBN: 978-1-4520-9873-9 (sc)
ISBN: 978-1-4520-9872-2 (hc)
ISBN: 978-1-4520-9871-5 (e)

Library of Congress Control Number: 2010917544

Printed in the United States of America

This book is printed on acid-free paper.

Certain stock imagery © Thinkstock.

Contents

A note from the Author

As you journey with my family and me through the world of schizophrenia, keep in mind that the individuals in the story are real. Included is all of what became and is a part of the structure of our family. It is my firm belief that members of a family share in the illness of any one member of a family who suffers with an illness.

This book was born out of a keen desire to be obedient to the will of God for my life. God put it in my heart that there is someone who needs to hear my story about my life with a husband living with schizophrenia. When John became very ill I had a fleeting though that I needed to tell this story. On August 17th God assured me that I needed to be about the work of fulfilling His will for me. Through all of the storms of living with a husband with such a dreaded illness as schizophrenia, there was hope. Because of God's guidance I have presented most completely how I learned how to manage through the storms.

I knew that God was my help in the time of storms. I remembered that "Jesus loved me because the Bible told me so," and not only that I knew that He loved me because he had shown His love for me over and over again in every area of my life. Leaning on my own understanding was not an option for me in the storms.

No matter how difficult the journey became I knew that the Savior was always beside me. In case I am misleading you into thinking that I was always brave and in control, there were many times that I thought I could not survive or go on. There were times in the storms when I lay awake with tears streaming down until the pillow was wet with tears. But in the midst of it all God calmed my soul and my very sinew so that I could get enough rest and renew my strength for next day. He prepared me for each challenge that I had to face the many years of John's illness.

Once I experienced the vision on August 17th and God's will for this book to be written, I faced many challenges within myself. Challenges of doubt about what people would think of my family and me. I was deeply concerned about how John would be treated by people once they read his story. I worried that people would think I made the story up. Worries and concerns have paralyzed me so many times on this journey of writing. Worry and concerns have hindered my writing sometimes for weeks.

God's promise and His love for me are so great that I am still trying to take it all in. Most recently, I had a concern that troubled me and as I began to pray in the early morning I told God what was troubling me and then I said to Him, but You have so many other people to answer and so many prayers to listen to and answer that I should not trouble you with my concern. As I had this thought I then remembered how great God really is. "He is that He is" and that is enough for me. I am reminded of an old hymn title, *What a Friend we Have in Jesus*. The words to the hymn are:

What a friend we have in Jesus all our sins and griefs to bear

Jesus knows our every weakness, take it to the Lord in prayer

Oh, what peace we often forfeit, Oh, what pains we bear

All because we do not carry everything to God in prayer.

It is His will that I bring ALL my concerns and challenges to Him. I have tried to be faithful to the mandate of writing this book that God has ordained. Even when negative thoughts have come into my mind I have been restored to peace because Jesus cares for me.

This is not an analysis of the medical effects of schizophrenia, but rather a sharing of my life with my husband, who suffers with the disease. I pray that God may be glorified in the telling of our story.

Even as I think about my thoughts and fears while writing the book I am in total awe of how God works in my life and how He leads me in every way. I pray that you will read this book with your heart and your mind and that if there is someone that you know who needs to know about how God can make a way out of no way and how He is still blessing and answering prayer today as he did in the beginning, please share this book with them.

As you read, may the love and blessings of our Savior fill your hearts to try to understand the families that may be suffering with a family member going through the agony of this disease.

If you want to know more about this disease, schizophrenia, you can check the websites listed in the appendix.

Dedication

The writing of our story is dedicated to the two people in my life who have traveled on this journey with me over thirty years.

To my husband, John, I dedicate this book with all my love. He has, through the good times and the bad times, been a good husband. He has celebrated my accomplishments and encouraged me to go as far as I could in my education. He has loved me with a love that is gentle and kind. I say with all sincerity that my life would never have been as blessed as it has been had he not been in my life.

To our daughter, Melissa, I dedicate the book and thank her for all the joy she has brought into my life. Her letter of love the night she read the first few pages expressed her caring and love and I was and am deeply moved by the purity of her heart and the words in her letter. (The letter is in the appendix.)

My deepest appreciation to the following people, who have encouraged me, read the manuscript for me and prayed for me as I have been obedient to the call of God.

Dr. Mary Williams, my dear sister and friend, thank you for your constant encouragement even when I had doubts and concerns about what others would think of me and my family upon reading the book. Thank you, dear Mary!

Sylvia D. Evans, my mentor, how can I thank you for the love you extend to me in every way. Thank you for the sanctuary and the safe haven you provided for Melissa and me and for the love you have given to me.

Dr. Jackie Magness and Dr. Elisabeth Roslewicz - what would I do without your friendship and your love? You have been steadfast friends through thick and thin. You have encouraged and praised my writing. Thank you for reading the manuscript as I continued to write.

A special thanks to the following people who have supported my efforts, prayed for the success of the book, and encouraged me to be obedient to the will of God:

D. Fleet

C.F. Williams

Thank you to Lucia Perillan, my acupuncturist, and Philomenia Queen, my massage therapist, who are my sisters in faith. Thank you for helping me to mend when I was terribly broken. Your love and celebration of my writing has given me great joy and constant encouragement.

Introduction

This book was written to share with the reader what it is like for my family and me to cope with the diagnosis that my husband, John, is a person with schizophrenia. John and I have made our story public for readers who may have a loved one suffering with this devastating disease.

The reader will, we hope, learn about the schizophrenia first-hand from the person who suffers with this insidious and crippling disease and from his wife who had to cope with the illness. We hope that the suggestions John and I have shared will be helpful to anyone who is suffering with the illness.

John has endeavored to answer a number of questions. His responses to the questions are a part of the ongoing text. John's questions and responses are addressed in topic clusters.

Definition of Schizophrenia

Schizophrenia is a group of serious brain disorders in which reality is interpreted abnormally. Schizophrenia results in hallucinations, delusions, and disordered thinking and behavior. It is a chronic condition, requiring lifelong treatment.

Contrary to popular belief, schizophrenia isn't the same as split personality or multiple personalities. While the word schizophrenia does mean split-mind it refers to a disruption of the usual balance of emotions and thinking.

Mayo Clinic Staff, 2008

According to the National Institutes of Health, schizophrenia is a chronic, severe, and disabling brain disorder that has been recognized throughout recorded history. It affects about 1 percent of Americans.

NIH further states that people with schizophrenia may hear voices other people don't hear or they may believe that others are reading their minds, controlling their thoughts, or plotting to harm them. These experiences, declare NIH, are terrifying and can cause fearfulness, withdrawal, or extreme agitation. People with schizophrenia may not make sense when they talk, may sit for hours without moving or talking much, or may seem perfectly fine until they talk about what they are really thinking.

The symptoms of schizophrenia fall into three broad categories which NIH describes:

> **Positive symptoms** which are usual thoughts or perceptions, including hallucinations, delusions, thought disorder, and disorders of movement.

> **Negative symptoms** which are represented by a loss or decrease in the ability to initiate plans, speak, express emotion, or find pleasure in everyday life. These symptoms are harder to recognize as part of the disorder and may be mistaken for laziness or depression.

> **Cognitive symptoms** (or cognitive deficits) are problems with attention, certain types of memory, and the executive functions that allow us to plan and organize. Cognitive deficits can also be difficult to recognize as part of the disorder but are the most disabling in terms of leading a normal life.

Above are descriptions and definitions of schizophrenia in medical terms. John and I will give our definition and description of what schizophrenia is to each of us. To me schizophrenia is a crippling, ugly, insidious, and frightening illness. It is sad and it hurts every fiber of the body. It takes you to places in the deepest parts of yourself that you never knew were there. This disease comes almost from nowhere that one knows and proceeds to steal what was a vital and healthy life. Schizophrenia has no name and no cure. It sends the life of the family members into a tail spin such that there is the feeling it will never end. The scars of schizophrenia never go away, but the scars don't hurt every day or forever.

John describes schizophrenia as a foreign Entergy. He believes that the voices are not his, but rather a kind of mind control. He does not know who is controlling the mind, but he knows it is being controlled. When his lips move and say ugly demeaning words, he believes it is something outside of his body. John says sometimes he feels as if there is a sensation similar to static all over his body. He is no longer afraid of this feeling as he was in the beginning of the illness. John says, "September 13, 1975 will always live in my mind and that night will always be a part of what I will suffer with for the remainder of my life. I don't understand how this foreign Entergy can see through my eyes and talk to me and for me. How can they block what I am thinking and cause me to have mood swings. Schizophrenia has taken a part of my life that will never return."

Preface
Background

August 17th could have been like any other day in my life. The day could have been filled with decisions to make, cooking to do, errands to run and other important things; however, this particular day was not like any other day in many ways. Yes, the day began with some of those things that take place on most days. I got up early to take our dog, Braxton, out, water the flowers on the patio and sit for a bit in the patio swing to enjoy the beautiful morning sky and to thank God for another day in my life. This is often the time I give thanks to God for His mercies through the night. I thank God for granting me another opportunity to do His will in my life. It is my daily prayer each morning to ask God to let me be a light for Him and to allow me to help someone with a kind word or a smile.

Morning is a precious time to begin the new day for me. Braxton and I returned to the kitchen where he devoured his breakfast and, as usual, looked for more to eat. I prepared breakfast for John and me. I ate breakfast, cleaned the kitchen and went upstairs to get dressed to go to look for blinds for several windows in the house, go to a store to redeem a bonus coupon from a well-known men's store in Silver Spring. After John, my husband, and I left the men's store I went for my acupuncture appointment. The appointment was, as usual, both healing and relaxing.

Acupuncture has helped me in many ways. I am blessed to have a wonderfully warm and extremely well trained acupuncturist who has treated me for many ills. My first experience at Crossings, the Center for Healing Traditions was for massage therapy for severe neck spasms. The massage therapist relieved the neck pain and spasms during the first visit. I continued the therapy and not only did my spasms improve, but my back pain was relieved and my hip improved tremendously. After some time the massage therapist asked me to consider combining massage therapy and acupuncture. I respected her suggestion and immediately made an appointment with the acupuncturist. Acupuncture therapy in combination with massage therapy has given me greater relief from neck pain as well as lowered my high eye pressure, relieved acid reflux and, more importantly, given me a new outlook on my state of health.

I will continue with August 17th, the day that I believe was the beginning of changes in my life that would last a lifetime. At the acupuncture therapy appointment I shared with my acupuncturist that the doctors had recommended that I have my gallbladder removed. Lucia was very surprised and she proceeded to talk more to me about how she could treat the gallbladder. Lucia was surprised because I had not mentioned this condition to her before this day. She began to treat me for the gallbladder to help me feel relief. I expressed to Lucia that I did not want to have the surgery.

I was treated August 17th for the health of the gallbladder. After a serious hour of therapy with Lucia I felt a tremendous amount of relief. She explained to me the area she was treating and how it would give me relief. After the treatment I was scheduled to undergo a gastric emptying study at Holy Cross Hospital in order for the doctor to determine whether my stomach was emptying normally. Prior to the appointment I thought about the test for a few days, but had no dread because I, too, wanted to know what was happening with my digestion. The doctor told me the procedure would take 90 minutes to complete. The reason I gave lots of thought to the test is, in my mind I had to decide how I would spend the 90 minutes. I decided I would spend ninety minutes in prayer for after all I had prayers to lift to God. Often times I feel that I don't spend enough time in prayer so this was a perfect time to spend in deep focused prayer. The technician explained that I had to eat a cold hard-boiled egg with something injected so the scans would reveal the activity of the stomach. I was quite surprised that I would have to be on my back for the entire 90 minutes. My instruction was that I was not to move. The technician made sure that I was as comfortable as possible. He had me get on what looked like a long metal tray, he placed a pillow under my knees and there were little plastic trays on each side of the metal tray for my arms to rest. I was assured by the technician that he was nearby and that he would check on me periodically.

After the technician left the room I snuggled myself as much as possible and began to mentally scan down the prayer list in my head. I closed my eyes and began to pray for friends and family members, for the conditions of our world and for those in leadership. I prayed for those who were suffering in any way, those who were dying and those who were mourning a loved one's death. I prayed for healing of my daughter, Melissa, and for continued health of my husband, John. The technician came in to inform me that I had been there for 50 minutes and that 40 minutes remained. I heard the number of minutes, but did not open my eyes because I did not want to be distracted from my prayer vigil that was bringing me much peace and contentment. My prayers came easily and I moved from one person or situation to another in prayer. I calmly and peacefully returned to my prayer vigil for the final 40 minutes of the test.

The next time I heard the voice of the technician informing me that I now had 21 minutes left before the test was over. I decided I had prayed for everyone else and now it was time to pray for myself. After all, I, too, needed to give thanks for all of the mercies I experienced every day. After beginning the prayers for myself I was in tears within the first minute. I was crying uncontrollably and was not sure why. I never opened my eyes it was almost as if they were glued together. Within a few minutes God revealed to me that I had not done what He had asked me to do. I was puzzled, but I was able to ask God what it was I was supposed to do and had not done. God revealed very clearly that I was supposed to share the story of my life with my dear husband who was diagnosed with schizophrenia 32 years ago. He revealed to me that I needed to share because there are others who need to hear how I felt and how I survived in the midst of the storm of the devastating disease called schizophrenia.

I submitted to the will of God and promised Him that I would do my best to do His will. I remember thinking in my head that I would need help with this story because I was not sure that I could tell the story the way I needed to show His glory through my family and me. I was assured that I did not need to worry about the writing because He would lead and guide me when I needed help. I cannot describe fully what I felt, but the best I can say is I felt a great sense of freedom. I felt a sense of total commitment to the task I had been assigned. It would be a mistake to tell you that I did not have a feeling of nervousness mixed with many other feelings of fear and inadequacy even after God had assured me of His promise to be with me on this journey.

Leaving the hospital, I still had the calmness along with a sense of joy and gladness for the experience I had in the final 21 minutes of the test. Once I was in the car doubt and questions about the journey I was about to take bombarded my thoughts. I had many questions: did anyone need to hear the story of a woman who lived with a husband who had been diagnosed with schizophrenia, would anyone care and most of all "why are you telling family secrets." I even began to doubt that I had the experience and would people think that I had lost my mind and made the experience up.

It was an especially beautiful day when I left the hospital. The sun was shining and in a strange way the air felt fresh and new.

Normally, I am eager to share this kind of experience with John, but I did not share the experience with him that day. I'm not sure why I did not share with John except to say that I was still sure of the encounter with God and yet I felt conflicted in many respects. I actually shared with no one until Friday when I went for massage therapy with Philomenia. It was so easy to share with her what I had experienced the day before. All of what I had not shared until now came bubbling out. As I listened to my voice babbling in a high-pitched voice I began to feel a sense of euphoria, maybe because this was the first time I had truly voiced what I had experienced. I felt free within the deepest part of my being, free perhaps because I had acknowledged what was reality for me. After lots of sharing I was again certain that I must begin to follow what God asked of me.

For some unknown reason, perhaps a bit of a setback, I did not get to the computer until Monday, four days after the revelation. The setback may have been the time I used to try to visualize in my mind what and how I would begin. It is so much clearer to me that free will causes me to stray from the course even though in my mind and my heart I know what God had willed for me. Finally, I sat down at the computer to begin the journey I was told to begin. After setting up the computer and beginning to type, John looked over at me and asked what I was working on. I stopped typing and immediately turned toward John so that I could see his eyes and his expression as I began to share with him what God had revealed to me. As I was telling John I began to feel tears well up in my eyes. I think the tears welled because I realized that He had tried to tell his story about a year ago and now God was using me to tell his story through my life (even as I tell you this now I am crying because I was the one to whom John had began to dictate his story. It is awesome how God uses each of us. I am thankful that I can hear and open my heart to His love and will in my life). After I shared God's revelation to me, John looked at me with a great sense of pride. He has a very special way of looking at me and acknowledging that he has heard me when I have something serious to say. I felt at this time that I needed to ask him did he mind if I wrote the story; after all, this was his story, too. He looked at me with great dignity and happiness and said, "I don't mind if you write the story, write the story."

Each night I have worked hard to set aside time to write. Sometimes when doubt sets in I take time away from the writing, but try not to allow too many nights to go by before I am back to writing. Each night or day of the weekend that I sit down to write, the words just keep coming. The words take life as I move my fingers across the keyboard. God is true to His word, how can I ever doubt Him. I am not bombarded with ideas or thoughts about what to write; it all begins when I begin the work for the night. One thing that does break through sometimes while I work is the negative thoughts about what people will think of me. I reflect on it a lot and always come to the realization that this task is not about people, whoever they may be, but all about the task set before me by God. Philomenia, my massage therapist, said to me, "What people think about you has nothing to do with you."

Chapter 1

Growing Up In Monroe, North Carolina

It is time for me to begin to tell the story of our early journey in the world of schizophrenia. This story really did not begin August 17th; it really and truly began 63 years ago. Sixty-three years ago I was born in Monroe, North Carolina. John was born in March nine months before I was born in November 1944. Our parents knew each other, but John and I did not know each other until we were 5 or 6 years old. We knew each other from attending the same church and then from attending the same school and most of the years being in the same grade together. John lived on Hudson Street and I lived on Paradise Street, about a block from each other's house. John was a brilliant student in school. He had a beautiful head (as he does today) and his tears were so big. I get tears in my eyes as I prepare to tell the following story.

During cotton picking season John had been out of school for several days or more and when he returned to school he did not know where we were in our lesson nor did he know what he was supposed to do. Ms. Chambers, our third grade teacher, yelled at John and as I carefully watched him, the tears began to flow because he was hurt not only in his heart, but he was embarrassed. He cried and sniffled for a bit and then sat in his chair and tried to focus. At that early age I wanted to cry with him because he had a bit of my heart already. Cotton picking time was not fun for us. John's family members were great cotton pickers while my family was hard pressed to keep up with them. When we stayed home to pick cotton we got behind in school and when we returned to school it was always an adjustment. We got up early in the morning to get on the back of a truck to go to the fields when the dew was still on the grass. We were always half asleep. Once the sun came up and by the middle of the day I became very sick in the fields. Sometimes Momma would send me to the cotton sheet to lie down in the sun. We ate lunch and returned to the fields to work until sundown.

Picking cotton was hard cheap labor. For both of our families it was a way for our parents to try to make ends meet. As if that was not enough, John and I would run home after school, get in our field clothes and walk at least two miles to a cotton field near our home to pick for 1-2 hours. I tried to pick more cotton than John, but to no avail - he was a better cotton picker than I could ever hope to be.

We gave the fifty cents we made picking cotton after school to our Momma to get something for the family and sometimes they allowed us to buy socks, fabrics or underwear. Those were wonderful days in our lives, not because we picked cotton, but because we both felt proud that we were helping and we were in the same place at the same time.

It is difficult to tell our story without sharing a little about our families and how we grew up. I often say to John that my family was poor, but we did not know it and Momma always made sure that we had something to eat even if it was not chicken. My mother was the breadwinner in our family. Momma worked as a maid for white families. She worked long hard hours, but always made sure to be home when we got there even if she had to go back to work later. She would always have a fire in the wood stove and food cooking in the pots. Momma was the one who kept us children together rather than give us away to someone else, though she was often asked. Momma is the one who worried over her children. She made sure that we were fed and clean and she loved us.

Her mother, my grandmother, died when Momma was 6 years old. Momma did not remember her mother very much. She had two brothers and she was the middle child. She cooked and cleaned for her brothers because my grandfather worked on the railroad and was away from home a lot.

As I am writing I realize that as we were growing up, Momma never talked about the fun she had as a child. Most recently, I have heard her talk about the time her youngest brother had a cat and he went to bed and slept on the cat. The next morning the cat was dead. Momma and her brothers were close. Well, actually she was close to her younger brother, but in later years she and her older brother became very close before his death.

Momma always bought us something for Christmas and when she was unable to pay for something for each of us she would go to the store and tell the manager of the store if he would let her have what she wanted she would pay for it on time. She always made good on her word and people, black and white, respected and trusted her. They knew that she was trying to raise 7 children basically alone. The years were difficult for Momma and for us as children.

As children we never thought about life being hard. We knew that Momma was unable to buy things for us the way some of our schoolmates' parents could. The three of us who were the oldest picked blackberries and cressy (watercress) greens to sell so that we could help Momma make ends meet. This was not a hardship for us we actually enjoyed going out to hunt for berries and greens in the fields.

It was always hot when blackberries came in and we would walk a long way from our house to pick them. We would then come home to take them to the white families to sell. We sold a quart for a quarter. There were families that bought each time we came. As we have become adults and look back on our life we realize that we didn't always understand what was going on, but we did feel the sadness that Momma sometimes felt as she worried and stayed awake at night wondering where she might get money for food, rent and clothing that we needed. She sometimes had to put paper in her shoes because she could not buy for herself. There were times we children had to wear shoes with holes in them.

Mary Ann, the oldest child in the family, had the awesome responsibility of making sure that all of us were rounded up and got home together. There were other responsibilities she had that were too much for a little girl who was so afraid of many things in life. She had no choice about what she was expected to do. All of us were born at home and I remember once when one of the younger siblings was born, Mary (Annie) had to help with the birth. She was only 12 or 13 years old; she cried because she was so afraid of what was happening. She did not understand and she was oh, so afraid, but she did what she had to do.

Mary transferred a lot of unspoken fears she had as a young child into her adult life. At age 65 she continues to work through many fears. She has managed her life quite well, even with all that she has had to endure. Mary was the dutiful child while I, on the other hand, developed a strategy for listening to some of the things Momma taught us and followed a different path. I used what I thought was reasonable and discarded what did not seem reasonable. Momma always taught us, when we were children, that we could not trust friends. Mary believed this literally so consequently she has no friends to come by to visit her or ones that she can count on to call, go shopping or go out to dinner.

When Mary went to college she was so proud of herself that she once said "I'm going to be somebody." Momma interpreted this statement to mean that Mary thought she was better than the rest of the family. To this very day Momma speaks of Mary's declaration to be somebody in blaming terms. Momma always told us that we should not brag about what we accomplished, but rather we should let others brag on us. I never really understood this nor did I fall in line with that completely. I say that and I reflect and feel that I too continue to carry some of what I heard as a child. I am not one to share some of the special accomplishments I have made. I have never framed my doctoral degree or my master's degree diplomas. I think that I interpreted what Momma said to mean that you should not show off your achievements. Later years in my life I have learned that it is okay to accept praise from others without trying to belittle or explain the praise away.

Mary is the firstborn and I am the second child in a family of seven children. There were four boys and three girls. Our youngest brother Steven died of SIDS. We did not know that in those days, but from what I understand about SIDS that appears to have been the cause of his death. In those days no one tried to find out why someone died. That was the first of Momma's 7 children to die. Momma continued to lose her children to death, one after the other. All of our siblings died before they were 50. My oldest brother died in his early 40s and the youngest sister died before she reached 50. Momma has experienced some very difficult times in her life. Some mothers could not stand up under loss of all of their children. Mary and I are the two oldest and only living children.

I am not sure just when it began to happen, but Momma began to change toward Mary Ann and me. The closest I can come to figuring out when is when we became teenagers, but even more

> SIDS is sudden infant syndrome.

when we went to college. Momma, for reasons Mary and I have yet to understand, began to pit brothers and sisters against one another. Perhaps this was an attempt to have control over each child. The grandchildren and the in-laws feel distain for Mary Ann and me. They feel this way because of the mean things Momma has said about the two of us. I am not guessing about the mean ugly statements made about one child to the other because I have heard them from Momma.

Recently, I told Momma that it was time for us to change our lives. There are two of her children living and it is time to forget all things and forgive all wrongs. I told Momma that we should have a reunion with the three of us. She agreed to the reunion with Mary Ann and me to be held April 2009.

After the agreement Momma and I talked daily for two weeks. One night near Christmas I called Momma and she began to talk about a lot of old things that happened in the family. She blamed Mary and me for the family being separated. She began to tell me that our father, whom I really did not know, was seeing other women outside the family and that he never gave her anything to take care of Mary and me. She said that Mary and I cared more for my father than we cared for her. At this point I was beyond words so I did not make any comments when Momma continued to say that we thought we were better than her other children because we always say that we are Williams'. She said that her other children were sweet children and the Williams were the worst people in Monroe.

The following day I decided that I would share with Momma that Mary and I are Williams because she married our father. I wanted her to know that this is the reason for the reunion, a time to leave all that stuff behind. I shared with her that neither Mary nor I ever had a thought that we were better than our brothers and sister. In many ways this may seem a mistake, but I believe that I was to learn a lesson and that lesson would serve me well if I learned it now. At this time I am not sure of all I learned, but what I have realized and learned is that I must keep my heart and my sinew safe from Momma. I also realized that my dear mother is filled with hatred, anger and sadness and that only a miracle can remove the hatred, anger and sadness she feels.

When I was finally able to say to Momma that I had to go, I was in a dark place in my life. I was broken, lonely and extremely sad. I have not and have no desire to share the entire ugly mean words Momma hurled at me over the telephone. However, I shared with John a little of what I had experienced. In his special way later that night he looked at me and said, in a gentle way, "You know you can't have a relationship with your mother, do you understand that?" I understand that it is dangerous to have a relationship with Momma whether I desire one or not.

Momma wrongly truly believes that Mary and I think we are better than our brothers and sisters. Most of my nieces and nephews believe that we have lots of money because we are teachers. The saddest thing about all of this is that Momma has only two children left and she is not close to either of us. Mary and I continue to help Momma as much as she will allow us to help. Many times we ask if there is anything we can do for her and her answer is almost always "No, dear, I am fine." Momma had a stroke four years ago and sometimes she loses things or forgets things, but she continues to say "no" to our offers of help. On special days she prefers money rather than a gift from us.

> How does one manage this kind of sadness except but to take care of the heart and mind? It is a sad commentary on the sadness that one suffers and never reconciles the sadness and grief they might feel. If I could change anything for momma it would be to give her joy and peace unspeakable.

When I go home, Mary and I pick Momma up and take her to the cemetery to visit family members, and then we take her for lunch. The last time I went home we did the same thing for the second time and Momma seemed to truly enjoy the ride and the talk.

Our discussions are always light. Mary does very little talking when we are together. She can no longer drive her car so she is homebound most of the time. It is also so sad that Mary is afraid to be with Momma because of the abuse she has suffered and because she never knows what Momma might begin to talk about.

John and I have been the subject of many talks Momma has had with the family as well as other people. I have not lived near Momma so she really does not know the person I have become. She does not know the granddaughter or son-in-law she has missed getting to know. Though we have gone home yearly and sometimes several times each year since Melissa was born, I don't believe that Momma would change her mind about us. In the beginning when I went home to visit it was very difficult to be who I was becoming as an adult because I always felt that I had to please Momma by being the little girl she continued to see me as. Over the years I have learned to walk in my shoes no matter what Momma thinks about me.

Nearly ten years ago Momma decided to leave all that she owns to her two granddaughters. They have the legal right to make all the decisions for her. When I tried to explain to Momma that it was fine if she wanted to do that, but what she had done was take away the opportunity for Mary and me to make any decisions for her if she gets ill or if she dies before us.

She said that is the way she wanted it. We were to make no decisions about her if she died. We were not even to make decisions about what she would wear nor take a part in her funeral services.

Mary and I do not, for one moment, pretend that we have not felt this deeply, not because we want what Momma owns but because we have no say for our own mother. However, we have had to accept what is fact. Mary often says to me if that is what makes Momma happy then I am happy because I want her to be happy.

I have included all of this background information because I believe it critical for the reader to understand more about me as a person and to understand something about my early life. If I were to write all about my early life it would be a book in itself.

It is important to say that Mary and I know that it is possible that over the years of neglecting herself and raising 7 children, Momma has grown bitter and resentful. This is a part of my life that I have prayed a lot about and about 15 years ago I prayed to God to take care of it because everything that I tried was wrong. When I tried to fix things in the family it has always become something ugly and every family member was encouraged to believe that I was trying to show off. I am satisfied to leave it with God.

I love my mother, after all, she is the person who loved me and cared for me and she is my mother. Mary and I forgive Momma for all that she has said or done. We would do and are doing things to make her days easier. I suppose some might say that we should overlook what Momma says and what she does and continue going over to talk to her. Personally, if I were to do that I would cross over.

An example of Momma's anger surfaced recently when she called Mary to tell her to pick up a chair and a hutch she had given Momma. She said the reason was that if something happened to her (death) there would be no reason for Mary to come into her house. I am thankful that we were not separated by all of the turmoil and dysfunction that took place in our childhood.

It is appropriate to share a dream I had many years ago as a very young child perhaps 10 or 12 years old. One night I had a beautiful dream of my sister Mary and me going down a long street that was paved with a kind of pavement I had never seen. The street was clean; in fact, everything was clean on the street. We were dressed in white dresses and white socks. As we walked almost in a floating motion on the street we saw many churches along the way. We stopped at churches on the left and the right and we heard beautiful choirs singing hymns and gospel songs.

I am not certain how long the dream lasted, but when I awoke the next day I remembered the dream clearly and still do now as I did so many years ago. The dream ended with the two of us still on the street that was so beautiful; I don't know how this dream could be interpreted, but I have often said to Mary that I believe a part of the dream was God's way of letting me know that we would not be separated and that we would have each other.

My childhood was not always easy. My father, I was told by Momma, left the family before I was born because he did not think that I was his child. At age 13 my sister Mary and I were walking down Hudson Street and I saw my father for the first time. He left us without looking back. How can I love a father I never knew?

Chapter 2

John And His Family

John is from a family where the children are all scattered and many of them do not talk to each other. John is the second child in his family. Richard is the youngest of 7 children and the only one who keeps in contact with all of his siblings. John had a very difficult and traumatic childhood. He has shared with me times when his mom locked him in the bathroom in the dark. He has also shared that his father was unhappy about giving mother money to buy food for the children. His parents fought a lot and this was something John watched and felt helpless to do anything.

Actually, there are so many things that are similar in our families. John in similar ways was alienated from his brothers and it appears that they don't trust one another. John and his older siblings do not communicate any longer. There was a time when he came to visit for a few hours, but over time the relationship has eroded to nothing.

The members of John's family don't understand the disease with which John suffers. What is more disturbing is there is no attempt to understand schizophrenia. They don't know his journey to hell and back. They don't know the times he has been admitted to the hospital. I tried to explain schizophrenia to one of his brothers who was totally unwilling to accept the fact that there is an illness called schizophrenia. Mary, my sister, has been the only family member who has supported John and me throughout the journey of our lives.

Chapter 3

Support In The Storm

The journey we have been on has been mainly without family support other than that of my sister Mary. Out of a desire to have my mother to talk with and to have her give me an encouraging word I made the mistake of telling her about John's illness and I have lived to regret that I did because she has held it against John for more than forty years. Even as I tell this part of the journey I shed tears and my heart hurts for the lost love and support from Momma and other family.

> It is difficult for anyone who has not lived with a person with schizophrenia to understand what happens to the individual.

I never really thought about it until now that Melissa, our daughter, John and I were mainly alone, but for the loving friends. Sylvia Davenport, my mentor, was a rock for me so many times. To this day she continues to lift me. She always knows what to say to me. Every time I talk with her over the telephone I feel extremely blessed and energized. I kept so much of what was happening to our family and especially to me. I went to work so many days not knowing what I would find when I returned to the house.

I returned to work after a year and a half and had to leave Melissa home with John. He called or maybe I called him and he asked me "what do I do with her?" I went home to get her and took her back to work with me. Later at one of our therapy sessions I related this to the therapist and he said to me that I could not leave the baby with John when he was so ill because I might come home and find her dead and John not realizing what he had done.

I called Melissa "the library baby" because she spent so many hours with me at work. When she was a baby I carried her in the baby seat and as she grew she sat on the floor near me or in her stroller while I went about my work and did storytelling programs at Noyes Children's Library. My supervisor, Nora Caplan, was loving, understanding and caring and she allowed me to continue to bring Melissa to work with me.

No one really knew what it was that kept me going, but I have no trouble knowing that I was not alone. Melissa grew up with her father ill and in and out of hospitals. There is so much that she did not understand and I did my best to help her to grow up strong and sure of the inner strength she possessed that would allow her to survive in the world.

She went to the hospital with me to visit her father. When she was a toddler she accompanied me on the drive to Taylor Manor Hospital in Ellicott City to visit her father. She sat in her car seat as happy as a lark to be with me. She really did not enjoy the visits to see her father and was always happy to be back in the car on the way home. Sometimes as we traveled up and down the highways I would laugh with her and talk with her, but my mind was always on several levels at the same time. I made sure that when dad was away, sometimes for months at a time, that I fed her and loved her and took care of her needs.

Melissa has, I believe, grown up secure, but has seen and gone through a lot in her life. I pray that what she has been through with her father and me has given her the strength she needs to become all that she can become. When Melissa was born I asked her doctor if she would be a person with schizophrenia like her father. His reply to me was, "Mrs. Covington, all you can do is love and care for her like you would any baby because that is a question that cannot be answered."

Chapter 4

Our Marriage

Little did anyone know that John and I would become best of friends when we were growing up. We attended Sunday school, Vacation Bible School, elementary, middle and high school. We picked cotton in the same fields and we were even members of a gospel singing group that we initiated. Many people find this hard to believe, but John and I never dated while in school. He called me almost every night after school to ask if I needed his help with homework. He wanted to make sure I did the math correctly.

From the very beginning I knew that he had a beautiful pure heart. John knew that I was not very good in math so he made sure that I understood before I came to class. We had a math teacher who sent us to the board to complete math problems. John saw me cry when I did not understand or had difficulty with a problem. He had feelings for me much the way I had feelings for him when he was in Ms. Chambers' class. I was extremely shy in school which made it painful for me to work at the board in front of the class. He asked if I needed help with French, but he was the one who needed help with French. I prided myself on the way I was able to speak the language and conjugate the verbs. Actually, John called to help me, but it was also an excuse to talk to me and me to talk to him. I enjoyed and looked forward to his calls as much as he enjoyed calling me.

I have vivid memories of the school playground and how I always kept an eye on where John was. One beautiful sunny day when we were in the third grade I looked across the field and saw him running across the field and in my mind and heart I said I was going to marry him. It sounds unbelievable that I thought that I would marry the man who has now been my husband for 41 years. I always felt so happy that he was where I was at church or at school. When he was not at church I missed him and always wondered where he was.

When I was in middle school I cleaned house and cooked for the music teacher, Mrs. Allen. When it was time for the musical concert John would come to Mrs. Allen's house to practice a solo or a group song on the same days I worked. I was extremely shy when he was around. We always made sure that our eyes met sometime during the practice.

In the eleventh grade John left Monroe to live in Winston-Salem, North Carolina. I did not know when he left and I did not have a chance to talk to him before he left town. It seemed that it took forever for him to come back to Monroe. He did return to Monroe during our senior year. He finished school as the valedictorian of our class. After we were married I asked where he had gone and he told me that he was in Winston-Salem with his mom and his uncle. When he returned to Monroe my heart was happy. When we were about twelve years old we both joined the church on the same day during Vacation Bible School. We were baptized on the same Sunday. John made my heart sing for many years before our marriage, July 28, 1968.

Digress: Tonight: September 3, 2007 John and I were watching the news on TV when the newscaster stated that a young man killed his sister. I said to John, the young man probably did not know what he was doing. I then shared with John that when he was very ill I left Melissa with him while I went to work for four hours. When I arrived at work you called me to ask me what you were suppose to do with her. I also shared with him that I later talked with the therapist about this and the therapist strongly advised me not to leave Melissa with you at this time because I might come home and find Melissa cut up or harmed and you not really knowing what you had done.

John's reply was who told you that, when I replied the therapist, his response was loud and clear. "He is a liar; he (the young man who killed his sister) knew what he was doing." My reason for interrupting the writing was to say how very real and yet immensely confusing this illness is because sometimes John says to me the "voices" made me do this or that or that they confuse me. In this case he was telling me that the therapist was wrong and that the young man who had killed his sister "probably" heard "voices," too.

Chapter 5

First Signs Of The Illness

John and I graduated from high school in 1963. John went off to Morehouse College and I went to Winston-Salem College. Neither of us knew quite what we were going to college for, but we knew all of our high school days that we wanted to attend college. After all, Mary had gone to college and I knew that I had to follow my big sister. Neither Mary nor I had a suitcase and we had very few clothes and little underwear. We went to college anyway because we had a teacher who believed in our abilities to succeed.

John, however, had a big strike against him before he even went off to Morehouse. When he asked his dad for money for college his dad asked him why he wanted to go to college. He told John that he had not gone to college so why did he, John, need to go to college. Well, we both completed our first year of college. John finished on shaky ground; so shaky that he decided to give up college for the US Air Force. He joined the US Air Force and was stationed in Germany.

John had an allotment taken from his check to send money to his mother to support his siblings. His mother did not use the money for what it was intended to be used. She used some of the money to buy alcohol to drink. John really felt that leaving college was the answer to the problem of buying clothes, food and keeping a place for his younger brothers and sisters. He put his life on hold to help his mother support the family. John kept some money for himself through Savings Bonds he purchased every payday. He sent them home for his mother to put in the bank. After being discharged from the service he came home to find that his bonds had been cashed and the money spent. For many years after our marriage John's heart was broken due to this misfortune. He later learned to release and let it go because it was gone and there was nothing he could do about it.

After being discharged from the USAF John left Monroe to work in Brooklyn, New York. He lived with his uncle and his aunt and their children. It was a wise decision for John to leave Monroe because there was nothing for him to do in Monroe. He had dreams and ambitions that he would be hard pressed to realize in such a small restricting town. He landed a job at Manufacturers Hanover Trust Bank in New York City where he was still working when we got married.

During the time John was in Germany we wrote to each other almost every day. Our dating was via the mail and the telephone. John shared with me that he had a rough time in Germany. He was lonely and so far away from the people he loved. He had also made the transition from college to the Air Force without time to reflect on his college experience. Once he came home on leave from the Air Force and he came to the college to visit me. I was much more than excited about his visit, but I was also nervous and afraid to go off campus to his uncle's for the evening. I did go and had a wonderful time. I was always sad when I had to say goodbye to John.

I missed him as soon as he was gone. While he was in New York, I was working my first year out of college as a librarian in Danville, Virginia. John never proposed to me and he always tells the story that I asked him a question he could not answer. That question was, we are spending so much money talking to each other by phone and I am missing you so much, why don't we get married. He declared that he had nothing to offer me and that the wedding ring would have to be a cigar band. I told him that I didn't care. Following that conversation it was not long before I found myself on a bus on the way to New York to visit John and to plan our wedding. No, we did not have an engagement nor did I get an engagement ring. We went to Battery Park in New York near the water to set the date for our wedding.

When I think about that time in my life, it was nothing new to me because it was what I wanted almost all of my life. John and I were content to sit on a bench in Battery Park and make a decision that would change the course of our lives forever. It would change our lives in ways that we could never have dreamed. John stayed in New York while I returned to Virginia to complete my first year of work at the high school. We met in Battery Park March 1968 and were married July of the same year.

When I talked to John on the phone I told him what plans were being made for our marriage. Mary, my oldest sister, and I went to New York to work as sleep-in maids for the last time that summer of 1968. We bought my gown in White Plains, New York at Korvette's Department Store. After buying the gowns, I saved enough money to buy my veil and my shoes. Mary and I bought the invitations and I addressed them in the evening after work.

John and I decided to have a very small wedding, but that was short lived when I told Momma. She told me that people were upset that we had not invited them to the wedding. John and decided to gave a general announcement to the church that everyone who wanted to come could attend. When I told Momma that I was getting married she replied that she would not come to the wedding. She did not want me to marry John. When Momma said that she was not coming to come to the wedding, I thought that my heart would break. I think that I had a breakdown, but I am thankful to God that He brought me back to my senses so that I could continue to plan for the wedding.

The wedding party that was planned became a nightmare when my oldest brother, Samuel, began to fight John. We left the party and were driven around by a friend until we could settle ourselves. We were shocked that Sammie would do this. Mary bought a beautiful cake and we were to have a simple reception. John and I took our vows. All I remember thinking was that I wanted to get married and leave Monroe as soon as possible. I left the church, went back to Momma's, changed clothes, packed a small bag and left Monroe with John and his uncle to go to Winston-Salem, then to our new home in Brooklyn, New York. The most memorable time in our wedding was as I walked down the aisle, seeing John waiting for me and wondering would I ever get down the aisle to stand beside him. We both were focused and we listened to the vows and took them to heart for better or worse, through sickness and health.

Life truly began for John and me. He continued to work at Manufacture's Hanover Trust in New York City and I landed a job at a private school in Long Island. John traveled to work by train and I travelled by train and 2 buses to Long Island. I taught high school English at the private school and served as a librarian for five years. John, however, landed a job with a well-known computer company and began working October 1968. We found a

> *Fear has crept into my spirit as I am writing because I am ahead of myself thinking how John had begun to show little changes that were a part of the journey we were about to take.*

church that we enjoyed attending. We decided to join that church after visiting for some time.

John and I visited his sister almost every weekend. We took the train to her house and rode the last train back to our apartment on Bushwick Avenue.

John and I both love music. He, however, is a collector of many different things. John began collecting 45's and later, 33 1/3 records. We always had music in our apartment in Brooklyn. Weekends were our time to rest and walk down Broadway to buy another record for his collection that was growing by leaps and bounds. We still have those records after 40 years.

John also liked to drink beer. So he had his beer and his music and for four years in New York he was a happy man. John started a coin collection of mainly silver which he later sold and began collecting gold and platinum. Coin collecting gave both of us great joy. When John became interested in a hobby, I shared that interest with him. I was not and could never be as neat and organized with the collections as he. He always uses a clean handkerchief to place coins in the albums. We have a photo in an album that shows me standing with great pride beside his first coin collections.

Almost every day of the five years in New York John came home with a little gift for me. The gifts and flowers were given out of love and caring. He also bought shoes and fabric for me. I made all of my clothes in those days. I look back on those days of sewing and I wonder how I did all of that. It was nothing for me to buy fabric one day, cut it out the same day, sew and press the garment and wear it the next day. Just as I became interested in John's interest, he enjoyed with great pride the things I became interested in. He watched me sew and was very complimentary when he saw me in the finished garment. He also loved that I was a good cook. I made and still do make delicious cakes.

The work at International Business Machines began to take its toll of John after some years. He worked on the midnight shift and when he came home he was alone and unable to sleep. He got little to near no sleep, drank beer, and went back to work. He became exhausted and did not know how to stop or to take some time off. His exhaustion became serious in 1973. I began to notice that John was drinking more and more beer and getting fewer and fewer hours of sleep. He became moody and sometimes went out to drive alone for hours. I forgot to mention that we bought a car in New York after we received our driver's licenses. We bought a beautiful 1969 white cougar. I began to drive to Long Island. We rented a garage down the street from where we lived. We were able to drive wherever we wanted.

Sometimes John drove after he had drunk more than a few beers. When he drank beer he thought that he had control driving and I was unable to convince him that he did not have control. We had several accidents that could have been deadly. During our 5th and last year in New York, I began to notice little things about John that I had not seen before. I attributed the changes to the fact that he was working too hard without enough sleep, which was right, but there was something deeper and I could feel it, but could not put my finger on it.

Chapter 6

Acknowledging A Problem
After Moving To Maryland

John was given the choice by International Business Machines Company to transfer to Maryland from New York during that 5th year and he jumped at the opportunity. There were multiple reasons John needed and wanted to leave New York. He needed a change of setting and he also needed to see new faces, and a chance to start all over again. John and I never really talked much about the reasons he needed this move, but the words were unspoken. (I feel a sense of fear now because I remember that eerie feeling I felt that something was about to change in our lives.) He accepted and I also thought that certainly this was a great move for both of us.

We traveled to Maryland to purchase a home. We were in the process of purchasing a home in Long Island before John was offered the opportunity to transfer to Maryland. We bought the home we are still living in, the house we bought 35 years ago. We went back to New York and began to save like mad to close the deal on the house here in Maryland. When John and I want something and we need to save more money, we discuss the issue and how we are going to tackle it. We are very good collaborators and we enjoy bouncing ideas around until we come to an agreeable plan for both of us. Then we follow that plan even if we need to eat beans for weeks at a time.

John was, without a doubt, happy to have been hired by IBM. This company was known to take care of its workers. Our arrival in Maryland was uneventful except for the fact that we were ecstatic first-time homeowners.

We were the first in either of our families to become homeowners. We made lots of changes to the house and yard.

After moving to Maryland John was promoted to manager and that was special in many ways. At the same time it was the beginning of a terrible and frightening journey. No one would ever believe that the journey was so cruel and scary. I still shudder at the thought of what the journey was like for us. Before John became seriously ill I began to notice subtle changes in his behavior and his moods. He was grouchy and fanatical about most things. A year or more before John became seriously ill, I became pregnant. We both were ecstatic that I was finally pregnant. We had some difficulty conceiving, but we were so happy that we did. The baby was active throughout the pregnancy. We could feel her activity every day. She was especially active at night. I was well throughout the pregnancy with no problems until the end of the nine months.

July 1st I began to feel pain and saw a bit of spotting so John drove me to Washington Hospital Center where my doctor practiced. I was in the ninth month of pregnancy. When we arrived at the hospital the doctor saw that I had not dilated so he told me that this was my first pregnancy so I should go home and that I would return later. John and I returned home and for a few days we could feel the activity of the baby, but not nearly as strong as before. After four days I began to feel ill and we no longer felt any movement from the baby. We returned to the hospital and when the doctor examined me, John was whisked out of the room and I was given something to make me sleep. Before falling into a deep sleep I remember looking at the face of the doctor and the look on his face told me that something terrible was wrong. He broke the water and the fluid was black because the baby had begun to decay. I don't remember how long I was drugged.

When I awakened, John was with me and the doctor and the nurse were there to tell me that I had a stillborn baby girl. I looked at John and at that time we both began to cry uncontrollably. I don't remember how long I had to remain in the hospital, but sometime during the stay I remember asking the nurse if the baby had a lot of hair. She said that they were unable to tell because she was dead too long.

We were asked what we wanted to do with our baby and advised at the same time that the baby could be cremated. John and I decided that we would give her a name even though we had not seen her. We named our darling baby Patricia. Patricia had been a part of our lives for 9 months and she deserved to have a name of her own.

I truly believe this misfortune was the beginning of the stress that would take us to unknown territory in our lives and in our marriage. John and I came home and for the first time in our marriage we were unable to lean on each other. We each suffered away from the other in our own way. John said to me that I had left no room for a mistake in the birth of the baby. I think that he meant I never thought of not bringing the baby home to live with us. It was a devastating experience to come home without a baby that I had carried for 9 months. John returned to work and I rested a bit before returning to my part-time job.

We both seriously needed to heal, but continued to suffer separately. The day I had to dismantle the nursery I cried uncontrollably. John was at work when I did it, but I knew this was a task for me alone. Both John and I walked into and by the nursery every day. Seeing the room was too painful to leave it set up. When we returned to the doctor for the post-op examination John told the doctor that had he not sent me home the baby would be alive. For a long time John and I remember what this uncaring doctor said. He said to John, "You are the angriest man in the world." We both thought the doctor showed no sympathy for us as a couple, having just lost our baby. The doctor who delivered the baby never told us why Patricia died before birth.

John and I determined after a time of healing that we would try to have another baby. We were successful and I became pregnant about a year after having Patricia.

During this time John was having lots of difficulties at work. He was again on the midnight shift and not getting enough sleep. The beer drinking began to escalate nearly out of control. Each night that he arrived at work safely I felt a great sense of relief. He always did and he returned home each morning. John began to do strange things like getting on his knees and crawling to edge the lawn. Things came to a head for John one day when we were in the backyard. John began to talk to me, but it seemed that he was talking to someone else. I became frightened, but I was brave enough to say to John that we need help because something is wrong. He agreed that day that he needed help from a professional. I felt that he too was scared to death about what was happening to him. At this time, I, like John, had no clue about what was happening to his life and what we would experience for the next 35 years.

Questions and Responses from John

Question 1: Did you see your move from New York to Maryland as a solution or partial solution to the illness?

John's Response: I saw the move as a solution to the illness. It was a good way to start over again. I didn't like living in New York. I needed a change from everything and everyone.

Question 2: Were you agreeable to going to the charismatic healing service, or was it more that Barbara or someone else urged you to go?

John's Response: It was more that someone urged me to go. I would have tried anything then. I could not understand what was happening to me at that time. I went and I explained to people what I was feeling, but they just looked at me. They couldn't help me.

Chapter 7

Looking Everywhere For Help

Today I still cannot remember how I secured a psychiatrist, but we ended up at our first session with the first of many psychiatrists. Each of the psychiatrists affected our lives in different ways, both negatively and positively.

John continued to work at IBM under great duress and strain on his body and mind. Things at work were not good. He was indeed a manager in title, but there were unspoken limits and expectations which seemed to stress him greatly. Life was getting more and more strained for John and me as we walked on a tight rope. The psychiatrist John and I went to was a very nice man. He was qualified to prescribe medication and counsel us. John liked this doctor so he tried to comply with his advice. As we tried to find ways to work through the new maze in our lives, John's mental health continued to deteriorate.

It is curious to me that all kinds of people came into our lives from where I don't know. Every person gave advice to us about what we needed to do for John to be cured. One such incident was the man who came into our lives; upon his advice we ended up in someone's home in a circle with people speaking in tongues and all other manner of things over the two of us. As we were standing there in the circle, I thought to myself we have got to get out of here. John felt he was in a strange place as well. We did get out of there, never to return.

Another incident happened when we were invited to attend some sort of meeting at Constitution Hall where a person put his hands on a person with an illness and said some words and the person was to be healed.

John went up and they put their hands on his forehead, said some words I did not really understand and John fell backwards. When an illness such as John was later diagnosed with beset our lives, we became extremely vulnerable. Being vulnerable in this situation manifested itself in strange ways such as why would we follow someone to these places we had never been before and we did not know the people? We became vulnerable because we so wanted this thing to go away.

John and I were referred by another stranger who had come into our lives to a doctor in Chevy Chase. The doctor in Chevy Chase, we were told, was able to determine what had happened to John by taking snips of his hair to look for heavy metals or something. This, too, was to no avail. It was obvious that John was not to be healed in this way. We continued to go for therapy to another psychiatrist. John was very clever in all of our dealings with doctors. He convinced them that he was fine and that everything was great at home. I think that many of the doctors who counseled us were afraid of John. When he raised his voice to explain something no one challenged him, but rather his outbursts were tolerated.

> If you are faced with an illness like schizophrenia the best way to avoid becoming opening vulnerable is ask for advice from your doctors and trusted friends. They will help you to stay clear of roadblocks and people who may offer inappropriate advice.

DIGRESS

I am trying so hard to get to the time in our lives when John had the first breakdown. I don't know if my heart and mind don't want to open that chapter or whether I am afraid to open it again. I don't know where to place this, but I am going to enter it in sidebar.

Another frightening incident that happened to me is when John would sometimes sit at the top of the stairs, look down at the couch and say to me, "There I am in the casket." That was a feeling of fear that was chilling for me after because there was nothing, but a couch. I would shiver and say to John don't say that, there is no casket there. Over the year I heard about the casket many times. It is possible that John was hearing voices at this time, but we never thought of that and none of the psychiatrists had mentioned this before.

John continued to work under lots of duress. I became pregnant again in 1976 when John was stricken with the first severe breakdown. Of course, we both were extremely excited. I was three months pregnant at the time. The night of the first breakdown is as clear to me today as it was 35 years ago; clear and memorable being the optional words because nothing was clear that night. John and I had gone to bed. John was quite restless that night. He woke up yelling.

John got out of bed and began to yell and say strange things as he walked down the stairs. During this time I was pulling him back from the door, but he broke my grip. I don't know how I had the sense to call 911. I did call through my tears and fright for what was happening to the man I loved. John went to the front door and began to yell out to the world that he was Jesus Christ. He continued this in such a loud voice that the neighbors were awakened.

He continued to repeat over and over again that he was Jesus Christ. Finally, after what seemed to me a very long time the police arrived in our living room with billy sticks in hand. It seemed that the more I told them that John was sick, the more they continued to work at subduing him. At one point I got in front of the officers and begged them not to harm John. The reply was "please move out of the way so that we don't hurt you." It took four policemen to bring John to the floor to handcuff him. He continued to repeat over and over that he was Jesus Christ. They took John away in an ambulance and I was left in the front yard wondering what had truly happened in our lives. After he was placed in the ambulance I fell to my knees in the front yard asking God what had happened to us.

Each time I have to write about that night I feel the drain and fear I experienced that night. I feel a weakness in my knees, my heart pumps, and I feel totally helpless. I was unable to get John to hear me as I continued to attempt to help him. I was not embarrassed by what was happening because there was no time nor was there a need to be embarrassed.

I was three months pregnant with a husband who was seriously mentally ill. The police told me they were going to take John to Montgomery General Hospital. I went to the hospital, but was unable to see him because he was, as they termed it, too agitated to see me. I returned home that night and I think that I walked and moved in a dreamlike state, trying to remain sane. I packed clothes, toothpaste and other things he would need. I, of course, thought that I would go to the hospital see him and bring him back home.

John was in the hospital for a long while. He was sedated and when I arrived at the hospital I was still unable to see him face to face. I did see him from the window and he had the angriest face I have ever seen. He was extremely angry with me; he did not even want to see me. I continued to work and go about life as if things were going to get better. Little did I realize that things were going to continue to get worse for us. When John finally came home from the hospital he was still angry and blamed me for all that had happened. He did not remember what had happened. He was angry that I had had him taken to MGH. I tried to explain that I did not know what else to do. It made no difference at that time or any of the other times I had to commit him to the hospital. John was heavily medicated. He went back to work with lots of difficulty. The doctors at the hospital and the doctor he was seeing regularly did not advise him to remain home for a while. When John returned home he would not let me touch him. If I tried to touch him he would ask me "what are you doing?" I did not understand that he was suspicious now and thinking that I was doing something to him.

John and I continued to muddle through this time in our lives. We

---

I was surprised to find that even when I shared with the police that my husband was ill they came to our home without a psychiatrist to counsel John and me. I was horrified that he was treated in such a criminal manner. It seems to me that there should be a person who accompanies or follows the police to talk with the patient and the family. There was one officer who told me the hospital where they were transporting John. I was left standing in my front yard with no one to advise me or to talk with me about the process John would go through. I managed to get myself together and get to the hospital that night.

---

continued going to a psychiatrist and John continued his medications. In the meantime I was, because of the previous stillborn baby, a high-risk future mother. John and I seemed to manage well with all that was happening, but underneath I knew we were on thin ice. John and I managed to go to all of the appointments and to look forward to our baby. There were many appointments and tests. We changed doctors after the mistake made by the previous doctors. John was careful with this baby, which was so different from the first baby. He was cautious and careful not to give his heart away.

Questions and Responses from John

Question 1: What were the symptoms of your illness that you first recognized? Explain where and when you noticed them.

John's response: One night at work I was unable to concentrate, I couldn't do anything. I was sweating a lot; I was disorganized and I finally just stopped working.

Question 2: When were you conscious that something was really wrong with your body chemistry?

John's Response: One Saturday night at work I thought of Barbara and the baby. I thought that the baby and Barbara were in danger. I began walking up and down the stairs and outside the building. Finally I left the building, without telling anyone, to go home to check on the baby and Barbara. They were fine. I remember Barbara said to me I was afraid something like this would happen. By the time I returned someone had called my manager. He was there but he did not ask me anything.

Question 3: What were some of your first attempts to cope with your situation at home and at work?

John's Response: I stayed up at night, drank beer all day and part of the night. I tried to work on an appraisal I had to complete. I usually went to bed around 1-2 o'clock and slept all day. I was not aware that I was ill. I thought it was me out of control. I found out later that I was out of control.

Question 4: How did you try to explain to yourself your insomnia and need to drink beer? Did you try to explain it to Barbara? Did you ever mention your insomnia to people at work?

John's Response: I guess I was an alcoholic at that time. I drank beer, wine and other spirits. I never mentioned it at work that I could not sleep. I got up every day, went to work and did the best I could. As a manager I guess I was all right; I functioned. After a while as a manager I was unable to concentrate. I was unable to complete projects I set for myself.

Question 5: Was there something going on at your job, stress or pressures that made you want to blame your illness on it?

John's Response: There was nothing at work to blame the illness on. Stressful, but I don't blame that on the illness. I blame it on the death of our baby, which hit me hard. I did not know how to handle it. I tried to work and forget about it. I didn't forget about it because it came back when I was working. I did not talk to Barbara. I missed the first child very much. When I found out that she had died I couldn't do anything but cry. When I took Barbara to the hospital I prayed to God that the baby and Barbara were all right. They were not all right. The death of Patricia broke the camel's back. After the death I could not focus. I could not work. I could not function and I could not concentrate. I blame the illness for showing its head at the death of Patricia.

Question 6: When and where were you when you first admitted you were seriously mentally ill?

John's Response: I was never aware. I thought it was something I could handle. One day coming from Dr. Weiss's office I was pulling out form Dennis to Georgia and something said something to me. I heard a voice. I have had voices ever since that I don't claim to be my own. They are with me day in and day out. I don't know how to stop them-they are a part of me now. When I die I hope they go away-I pray they will. They influence my thoughts, change my moods, influence my opinions and they are a hindrance and a nuisance to me. Now I just ignore them as much as I can.

March 2, 1976, I began to experience the same symptoms as with Patricia, our first baby. John called the doctor who told him to bring me into the hospital right away. We had everything packed and John made sure that I had a pillow. Only God knows how he was able to do all that he did with so much medication and being so ill. His love for the baby and me was greater than the illness he was suffering. John took me to the hospital in the morning and Melissa was born March 4, 1976 at 1:58 that day. The doctors wanted to see if it were possible for me to deliver Melissa without the planned C-section. They were willing to let me try until they saw that Melissa was in distress. When Melissa began to show stress, the doctors started the process of giving me an epidural. This procedure is quite painful and I had lots of trouble with the procedure, so much so that when the cutting began, I felt the knife and remember saying to the doctor "something is hurting me, what is that?" At this point I was given something to help me not to feel the pain.

Melissa was born and I was able to see and hold her immediately. She is our blessing. Wrapped up in her was all that we had missed with Patricia. I'm not all together sure if this was good for Melissa. John and I were elated that we had Melissa. It's not as if we ever will forget Patricia, but here she was our second chance at the blessing we had missed with our first child. She was and still is very beautiful! She had a head full of hair, tiny little lips, all ten fingers and toes, and beautiful eyes. How could John and I ask for more? We did not ask for more.

It was an hour or maybe less when the doctor rushed into the room to ask John, who was probably more alert than I, to sign a paper to give the doctors permission to give Melissa an exchange transfusion. My blood and her blood had mixed, but were not compatible. John was, though no one knew, very ill at the time, but he consulted with me and we made the decision to sign the paper. We were not sure of all the implications had John not signed the paper, but we understood that if she did not receive the transfusion she would be brain damaged. Melissa was under the bilirubin light for some time. She had the exchange transfusion and bounced back quite well. It was a day or perhaps the same day I was able to feed Melissa. We were in the hospital for 6 days and nights.

Though John was excited and thankful, I was aware that driving to and from the hospital from Wheaton was beginning to take a toll on him. It was on the 6th day that I told the doctors that I had to go home. I was sure that John would take good care of the two of us as sure as I knew the stress of driving to D.C. was too much for him at the time. John picked

Melissa and me up on a snowy day, March 10th. It was beautiful outside, as beautiful as that little bundle we carried home. Those were the days when there was not a law that babies had to be in a car seat. I dressed Melissa in "lots" of clothes, a hat, socks, booties and a heavy blanket. She was dressed and covered in so many clothes that I was afraid I would drop her. She was very warm, so much so that she was damp by the time we got her home.

Our home would never be the same once we had Melissa with us. The house was filled with joy unspeakable. The joy of having baby Melissa grew each and every day. I experienced life in a new way. As a baby Melissa was not a good sleeper. She took more catnaps than she actually slept. She enjoyed being near me. Because she did not sleep well, I became extremely tired and unable to concentrate. When I spoke to the pediatrician he suggested that we put a portable cart in our room so that she and I could get some sleep. Out of desperation I immediately got a cart and put it on my side of the bed, hoping that we both could get some sleep. It worked! Melissa slept well every night and so did I.

John and I always took Melissa with us everywhere. We took her to the zoo, various parks, the circus, Disney World, Busch Gardens and many other special places we enjoyed together. Melissa had so many interests and talents. She loved to write poetry and draw. She learned to read at an early age. We always read books in our home and she heard me tell stories from my mouth. Melissa and I spent time in the kitchen together; when I cooked, she cooked also. She had a little stove, oven and sink in one corner of the kitchen. She set up a little school with her toys and dolls and Curious George. After she put her food on the stove to cook she would turn around and teach the toys and dolls. She always asked for the scraps from what I was preparing to cook in her kitchen.

There are so many things I could continue to tell you about this special little girl, but at this point I need to speak to some of the other things that were taking place in my life.

There were other reasons our house would not be the same. John was becoming sicker as the weeks went by. I was working part-time at a Montgomery County Public Library when John continued to grow ill. He had to take disability retirement because the "voices" he heard in his head had become more real, making it extremely difficult for him to concentrate and remain focused. John suffered daily with "voices" that were discouraging him in anything he attempted. In the beginning I did not understand the insidiousness of "voices" but as the years went by, I began to understand more about the "voices." When I say that I understood the "voices" more, that is not to say that I knew how to react at this time; it was later, with the help of Karen, our therapist, that I learned more about what I was facing with the illness John was suffering. John enrolled and attended Montgomery College to study to become a physical therapist. He did very well at MC the first semester making all A's. The second semester was terrible for John because the "voices" became stronger and more discouraging, so much so that it was impossible for John to retain or recall information.

During the time John was getting more ill I remember one night, September 13, 1975, we were asleep and I had what I refer to as an out of the body experience. I was asleep, and in a strange sort of way an observer at the same time. I saw a horrible figure coming up the sidewalk draped in a black cloak with a sickle in one hand. I said to the figure, "No, you can't come in," but the more I protested the more the figure proceeded toward our front door. At this point, I continued to scream no, you can't come in, go away. The figure without a face turned the doorknob on the front door and continued to walk into our living room with a deliberate slow pace. Finally, the figure began to climb the stairs to our bedroom. I became more and more frightened and continued to yell, no, no, go away. He came into our bedroom and on to my side of the bed. I remember yelling and ending up pushing my body up on the headboard and yelling so loudly that John woke up and began to shake me. Before I was completely awake the figure plunged at me, but I moved and it stabbed John in the heart. I was so frightened I could not move or tell John what had happened. I often wonder if John being stabbed in the heart was an omen of what was still to come in our lives.

Chapter 8

The Voices

Sometimes John shared with me what the voices said to him. I was so afraid of this unknown "thing" that was real and had become a part of our lives. Sometimes John would tell me the voices said he should kill Melissa and me. And he always said to me I would never do that. Sometimes John sat and looked into space for a long time, just listening to the foreign chatter that had invaded his head. The "voices" had become a real part of his life and consequently had invaded Melissa's and my life.

One day John, Melissa and I went to shop for groceries and as we were shopping I had my list and was asking him about purchasing something when he looked at me and said, "There is no need to buy too much, we aren't going to be here long." Given the fact that I was afraid of the "voices" his words meant only one thing to me and that was maybe the "voices" had won and maybe John would kill Melissa and me. I became so frightened that I grabbed Melissa up in my arms, left the cart in the middle of the store and went to the car. John asked, "What is it?" I was so afraid that I was unable to talk for fear I would stir the "voices." They had actually become real to me. As soon as I got home I went to wonderful neighbors who lived across the street and told them what had happened. I was hysterical by this time and Marilyn had to shake me so that I could hear what she needed to say to me.

John joined me at the neighbors and said that he meant nothing by what he said to me. I believe at the time that John did not understand what was really going on in his head. For me the "voices" had become a threat to me; they were invisible until words were spoken by John. I felt very frightened by something that was such a threat but I was unable to see the "something." It was some time later that John referred to the chatter in his head as "these voices." We got through that episode only for me to grow more and more fearful of John and what I did not understand. What I understood was very little. I knew nothing about "voices"; I had become confused and perplexed trying to figure out what was going on in John's head. There was no template for me to follow on this journey and there was nothing at the time to satisfy my confusion.

We continued to attend church though our lives were a wreck. John felt quite safe and comfortable at church. Perhaps this was due to the fact that he felt protected from what was happening to him while in church.

My advice to anyone who might have this illness in their family or who might be suffering with the disease of schizophrenia is to find a doctor to explain what it means for an individual to hear voices. Try your best not become so afraid that you are unable to hear the doctor explain.

Don't be fooled into thinking that it is not fearful. It is. The best way to get through the terrible times is to listen to the individual suffering with the disease and share this with the doctor.

I encourage you to think about going to a psychiatrist who will listen to you and the patient. When you go to the first visit, make sure that the doctor does not direct the conversation to you or the patient. You, the doctor and patient need to make an agreement that in the best interest of the family and the therapy sessions, everything should be understood by each member.

It is critically important that the patient understand that you are a member of the team and that you are sometimes better able to key in on times when the illness is not progressing in the right direction.

It is my firm belief that securing the right doctor for this illness is critical. Push to get this task done as early in the illness as possible.

Chapter 9

Medications

John has taken a multitude of different psychotic drugs. I don't think that he missed many of them on his journey to hospitals and psychiatrists. John was prescribed Clozoril, a drug that had proven to be a wonder drug for many who suffer with the debilitating disease, schizophrenia, but for John Clozoril was deadly. He became a walking zombie. While on this drug John would sleep all day and all night. He had little energy and no appetite. I went to work each day leaving him sleeping and returned to find him still asleep. I woke him only to see him in what is best described as a stupor. He did his best to attend to his hygiene, but it was difficult because he was so drugged all the time.

When he was on this drug, Melissa's class went on a trip to Costa Rica with her school. John and I traveled to Dulles Airport with another family because I did not know the way and John was not able to drive because of the effects of medication. He refused to stay home and not see Melissa off. It was difficult for me to leave him home when he was on the medication because I was always afraid he would hurt himself or fall down the stairs. The evening when we were to leave for the airport John got up, took his shower, got dressed and waited for the other family to arrive. There were times I had to help him to get down the steps or to get on the transport to the airport

If asked how I felt looking from the outside at my husband and father of our child struggle so hard, I am not sure that I can answer adequately because I am unable to respond to how helpless I felt. I continued to observe him being helpless until we were sure the medication was not going to work. When John was on Clozoril, I began to become his advocate with the medical establishment. It was for me a time when I had to really begin to speak up on John's behalf. His doctors sometimes said the reactions would go away over time. The fact was the doctors were not present when John suffered each day from a drug that was slowly killing him. Doctors are not the ones who suffer throughout the days and months waiting for a medication to work. I became quite angry sometimes when doctors prescribed medications to John and sent him home for me to work through the hard days and nights. Normally steps in a home are no problem, but for me there was constant fear that John might fall while I was at work.

After John's experience with Clozoril I became a stronger advocate for his health. It was easy for me to inform the doctor that John could not take this medication because it was killing him. Of course, we were told that the side effects would subside as time went on. He was taking the medication for three months and in that time he was unable to drive or concentrate. His doctor finally heard me and took John off the medication. John was prescribed a different medication that worked well for him for about three months. After the three-month period on the drug Prolicsin he began to get progressively ill again. During the first three months on the new drug John was able to function without a lot of sleep, he was not cross or snappy all the time. He shared with the doctor that the voices were quieter. During the first few weeks of John receiving the injections there were many days he sat, not listening to the "voices," but wondering where the "voices" were. The Prolicsin injections worked so well that I think John was confused about what had happened to the "voices" that had held him hostage for so long. He was alone and suddenly bothered by the silence in his head. The silence of the voices was short lived because the Prolicsin injections soon stopped working for John.

In the early days of the illness John's body would work fairly well on some of the medications for a short period of time, but sooner or later he would become more ill because the medication he was taking became ineffective. It was always a scary setback when a particular medication no longer worked. When the drug became ineffective I was always aware because by this time I had become alert to any changes in John's behavior. Sometimes John was aware and other times the illness was so insidious that he was not aware of the changes in his moods and behavior. Each time the drugs were ineffective he was beset with another setback in the illness.

Melissa was still a real member of this family that was suffering. Melissa interpreted what was happening in our home in her own youthful way.

When she was old enough, she remained quiet about what was happening to her father. She observed a lot and she was coping as best she could in her own way. John yelled a lot and sometimes I tried to match his yelling, especially when it affected Melissa. I was always aware that Melissa was present and I did not want her to hurt so I held a lot of anger inside.

Once Melissa put my wedding ring on her finger and asked if she could wear it to school. I gave her permission to wear it. Her interpretation to her friends was that I did not care because her dad and I were on the split anyway. I suppose one could interpret this many ways, but I said earlier that I did everything I could to protect her and maybe giving her permission to wear the ring was a strange way of attempting to soften what she was going through in our family.

John has lived with voices for more than 34 years. "They" have been a part of our lives for 34 years. The "voices" are not gone; "they" are still a part of our lives. "They" are not as loud some days as they are other days. Using the word loud to describe how active the voices are for John does not mean that I can hear them audibly, but the chatter is not controlling his mind as much. John always says to me that he can never let his guard down. When he lets his guard down, that is when "they" have more control over what he says and does. For example, when John drives, he may drive fine for a time and then all of a sudden he begins to drive as if he is racing. He explains to me that it is not him but "these things in my head" that cause me to drive faster. Yes, I am sometimes afraid to drive with him today because of this. He drives wherever he needs to go. Sometimes he will not drive when the "voices" are too loud. John is convinced that there is no medication or anything that can take away the "voices" in his head. He always tells the doctor that the "voices" will stay with him until he dies. He strongly believes that he must keep his guard up all the time so that "they" will not intrude into his life and cause him to do something strange or dangerous. John has to concentrate and focus at all times in everything that he does.

He has tried to stop drinking Coke sodas for a long time but when he is so sure he has kicked the habit, the "voices" tell him to go get another soda. Hearing this, many people would say, oh, he knows that he is telling himself to get the soda each time he has tried to stop. I, too, used to think the same thing and sometimes the old me returns and I say he can help it, but truly I know that he can't because the "voices" give him all kinds of reasons why he deserves a soda.

DIGRESS: I sometimes wonder when an individual who suffers with this disease gets confused after time as to what he/she is thinking and what the "voices" are saying to him. John determines what is real from what are "voices" by believing that what is good is of God so that is right and what is harmful is not of God. If you are confused I can tell you that sometimes I am still confused except to say that because John is a believer he has found, in his own way, with the help of the Savior to decide what is of God.

We all make excuses for why we should do one thing or the other that is not good for us, but the "things" in John's head hide or cloud his thoughts. He is trying to stop drinking Coke again, a necessary decision for more than one reason, but even today the "voices" try to get him to start drinking Coke again. John is a person with Type 2 diabetes, which means that soda should not be a part of his diet.

When John was severely ill and on lots of medication he remained as loving and caring as he was able to be with Melissa. He helped to make family decisions and take care of the finances. He wanted Melissa and me to have the experience of travel. While on the medications he drove to Busch Gardens, to Harper's Ferry, and we made it to and from each place we traveled. The question might be why I allowed John to drive while he was on so much medication. Actually, that is a fair question, but I am not able to answer it except to say that he felt able to do the driving and I, at the time, was not aware of the stress that it could have caused him. John too, was unaware of the danger of driving with so much medication in his system. This is another instance of God's mercy. I strongly believe that John desperately needed to be in control of what he could handle successfully because so much of his life was controlled by voices.

Nearly fifteen years ago when John became severely ill, the "voices" had taken over his life to a great degree. He would talk about things in the crawl space of the house, he became obsessive with the food and how I should cook and plan meals. When he prepared a meal he wanted Melissa and me to come to the table immediately. He had no patience for Melissa who, as an only child, always had input into the table conversations. I was beginning to feel as if we were wrapped in a blanket afraid to make a move. John was so extremely critical about everything Melissa and I did. He kept a very close eye on Melissa and me all the time. I was unable to go anywhere without telling him the exact time I would return. If I did not return at the time he expected he would make a fuss about it and want to know why I was late. Any reason for being late was unacceptable to John. In those days Melissa irritated him. She was a teenager with lots of interests to share. I always felt as if I was protecting Melissa from her father's undeserved anger toward her. She never understood and why should she because neither did John or I.

It was my duty to protect Melissa, who was loved dearly by her father, but she saw him as a monster and at the depths of the illness he saw her as an irritation in his life. Melissa was under a lot of stress; for this reason I had to forget myself in order to protect her. As she continued to mature, John seemed to become more resentful of her. He wanted all of my attention, which was impossible. Sometimes when Melissa was sick, as a baby, John would look at me and say, "I know a secret." I was always afraid that he would tell me something evil or strange that the "voices" had told him about Melissa. I never asked him what the secret was; in fact, I always managed to change the subject. Whenever he said this, I always felt as cold as ice. After all, what in the world would I do if he told me something that I could not manage emotionally? I was already emotionally drained.

I knew that John was getting sicker and I felt there was nothing I could do about it. By this time I was tired and totally exhausted with the situation I was living in. It seemed as if there was never an end to my fears. I use the word fear because that is what I felt in every fiber of my being. In my mind I was always thinking about what I could do to help get our lives under control. In many ways I thought that one day this would all be over because it would just go away as quickly and all would be well. The problem was the illness did not come quickly as it came and it did not progress slowly. The disease had come over many years and it was only a matter of time before it would show itself in this dramatic way.

The illness became so severe that I finally had to go to the judge to request that John be committed to the hospital. I thought that if John were hospitalized at the right place he would have a chance to get the medication dosages appropriate for his body. Committing John to an institution was one of the most difficult things I have ever had to do in my life and little did I know that this would not be the last time I would have to commit the man I loved and the father of our child to a mental institution.

I was in constant prayer and fasting when I had to find a place that would attend to John's illness. The hospitals he had been in prior to Taylor Manor did not work with John long enough to get the correct dosages of medications for him so that he could begin the healing process. John has been in day facilities as well as in-patient institutional facilities. None of the hospitals was adequate to treat John. Once he was in a hospital in Washington, D.C. where he walked out of the facility, got a taxi and came home. My neighbor was able to talk John into going back to the facility. Realizing that I had to do something, I began to search for a facility that would help John to have a better quality of life and help him to survive. I was sitting up late one night watching television when I saw an advertisement for a hospital in Ellicott City, MD. I thought I needed to check this place out to determine if it was the place to send John. The next day I called Taylor Manor and spoke with a woman there who was the answer to my prayer. The woman at Taylor Manor told me that she had just read a book by Phyllis Naylor and that she did not know me and there were no beds, but she wanted me to enroll John so that he could come the next week.

John had no choice about whether he should go or not because we both knew that he was getting progressively worse. At the time John was in a facility in Maryland because he had awoken one night and looked at me and said "Goodbye, Barbara." The tone in his voice was a guttural sound like none other I'd heard in my life. He was standing tall, looking wide-eyed, and coming ever close to me. As he was repeating this he continued coming toward me. I called Melissa and said we have to go. We barely got out of the house, I say barely because I don't really know if he was hallucinating or whether the "voices" had told him to say goodbye and to kill us this time for sure.

The night this happened I had forgotten to put my keys in the right place, but I had money and it just so happened that the jacket I pulled out of the closet had my keys in it. Melissa and I got into the car and drove to a hotel in Wheaton where we stayed until John was out of the house. That day I went before the judge to commit him to Taylor Manor in Ellicott City, Maryland for the second time.

Chapter 10

A Child Tries To Cope

When John was at Taylor Manor and Melissa was a little girl, I continued to work part time every day. I enrolled Melissa in a daycare near where I worked when she was three years old. We drove to Taylor Manor as many as 2-4 times each week. Melissa sat in her car seat telling me about what happened during morning at daycare. I did my best to focus on what her needs were as well as focus on the road. While trying to focus on her needs and the road I wondered what kind of mood John would be in that day when I arrived at Taylor Manor.

Melissa never showed any negative feelings about going to Taylor Manor and now that I think about it she probably felt safer when her dad was out of the house. She did not have to worry that he would yell at her or at me. I often said to John he was yelling, but he never accepted that he was yelling. I guess it is hard when there is something bombarding your thoughts all the time. Our visits to Taylor Manor were always difficult because John always wanted to come home. He could not understand why I committed him to TM and why he could not go home. Melissa and I stayed some days while he ate. There were other times that I cooked and brought him dinner or fruit or something I thought he might like. When the visit was over we said goodbye and left. Melissa never mentioned a word about daddy and what she felt. We got into the car and drove down the winding roads from TM back to our home in Wheaton. We always tried hard not to let the dark catch us. It was as if Melissa was glad that this was over and that she and I could go on living our lives without daddy.

Melissa, I think, has wiped a lot of what was happening to her father from her memory and perhaps this writing will help her to bring it back so that she too can cry and let it rest from her subconscious. Actually, I think that we store scary, frightening memories from our minds so that we can cope. I said earlier in this writing that God not only meant this book for others who might need to see His Glory through this family, but for me as well. While writing this book I have learned to cry again. I have also allowed myself to relive some of my deepest fears, hurts and disappointments I experienced in the midst of John's illness. I am facing some of the fears that I could not allow myself to feel.

From the beginning of the illness I have had lots of fears about many things that I was unable to control. Fear is negative, I know that, but I found it difficult to manage this ugly thing that had invaded our home and our lives without asking our permission.

The longer I lived with the emotions and what was happening to John I cried a lot. Suddenly one day I had no more tears to cry because they did not make things better. I decided to stop crying and never cry again in my life. I have learned that sometimes crying can help release the hurt one feels. I have been able to relive many of the some of the hurt disappointment and sadness that came along with the illness.

When I asked Melissa for her permission to continue on this journey of writing the book, she wrote me what I call a Love letter. In the letter she said that this would be a blessing for my family and for her family someday. Well, I'd like to say now that this writing has been more than a blessing for me; it has freed me to some degree, cleansed me and has allowed me to voice in this writing the Glory of God and His true love for me. I pray that this writing and the journey we are upon during this writing will help Melissa and John.

While Melissa and I hid in the hotel in Wheaton after leaving the house, it was difficult to be in the hotel while John was in the house. It is possible that we were hiding something inside about what we were truly feeling. I felt as if my heart was split right down the center. I was in the hotel with the daughter John and I loved and yet I felt that I needed to protect her from what could have happened. Melissa continued to go about doing what she needed to do to survive. We took clothing and other necessities to the hotel. The next day I bought other clothes for Melissa to wear until we could get back to the house.

Melissa went to school that Monday which was good because there she had friends who cared for her and classes that kept her busy. As I have continued to work on writing, Melissa has shut down on reading or sharing anything about the book. She has shared with me that at this time in her life she is unable to open this part of her life. She feels that she is dealing with other issues that are draining to her. Melissa assured me that she loved me, but could not bring herself to read beyond the first sixteen pages. It was not disappointing to me because I know that it was not meant to be personal toward me. Someday when she is stronger perhaps she will be ready to read. I am not sure how we as humans can block things, but I do know that Melissa must remember the times her father hugged and kissed her, read to her, put toys together for her, and even when he was terribly ill and unable to do yard work he went outside to play with her or sit and watch her play in the yard. Her father loved her then as best he knew how. He loved buying Barbie dolls for her and almost anything she wanted. Maybe Melissa could not understand how this loving father could also be someone she feared.

Melissa loves music today because in our house her dad played all kinds of music and she began to love and appreciate all kinds of music. I marvel at the things Melissa does that are so like her father. John collects African-American art prints and when he buys he always wants signed, numbered and dated prints. Not too long ago Melissa began to collect art, but "poo pooed" the idea of having prints signed, numbered and dated. Today, she collects African-American art prints and wants only the ones that are numbered, signed and dated.

After reading the first 16 pages of the book Melissa and I have had brief conversations about some of her memories. She told me she that when she was a little girl playing house with her dolls she always killed daddy off so that it would be only me and her. I am not a professional therapist, but I believe that she thought that it was easier not to have daddy around because she never knew what to expect from him. Perhaps she never felt safe with him. She also shared with me that she remembered the time that we visited Taylor Manor when they had a Christmas play for the families. She remembered the Christmas tree had green balls. She remembered that I stopped at one of the shops in Ellicott City before we arrived at TM and bought her something to eat and she got sick. She also remembered the time we visited dad and it began to snow. She reminded me about how afraid I was that evening because the snow kept coming and I was so nervous driving around those curves coming from TM. Melissa never mentioned anything about her father each time we left the hospital.

We got home safely that day. I think Melissa was not worried because she thought that I could do anything. I did a lot out of necessity, but I was scared to death a lot of the time, too. It makes me cry to think that Melissa may have thought that I could do anything because I did hold up not on my own, but by the Grace of God. I was scared beyond any words I can use to express to help someone else understand the depth of the fear.

Chapter 11

About Me

I think that many of the people I knew during the illness had no idea that I was so afraid, stressed and unsure of what had happened to my life. My dearest friend and mentor, Sylvia, gave me great comfort and reassurance of God's love and that all things would work out. I met Sylvia at a time in my life when I was broken, a time when I wanted to curl up in a ball and stay there forever. After John took medical disability from IBM, I was forced to go to work full time.

I was quite ambivalent about leaving Melissa, but she was in 6th grade and quite independent. She understood why I needed to go to work full time. I made sure that her dad and I were always there for her when she had any programs or school birthday parties. We had the summers and most of the same holidays at home together because my first full-time job was in the local public school system. Sylvia was my guardian angel from the moment we met. She seemed to know so much about me even before I told her. I don't think that she knew I had an ill husband, but she sensed it. I trusted her from the moment I met her and was able to share very freely with her about John and the loss of our baby. In fact, Sylvia was the first person with whom I was able to share openly that we had lost a baby to stillbirth. She looked at me that day and said, "That must have been hard." I, in my controlled manner, at the time looked away and said to her I can talk about it now. As Sylvia and I became more than just friends she was able to help me through some difficult moments in my life. She did not always have words or say words to me; it was her presence that was so strong and her faith in God that was so evident which made me feel secure in her presence.

One night when Melissa and I had to run (escape) from John, Sylvia was the person I went to first. I knew it was safe for us. I had time to reflect on what my next step was and how to execute it. We stayed several hours until the middle of the night. Sylvia is the friend who can tell how I am even before I tell her. I'm sure Sylvia knew there were many times I was thinking on several levels at the same time. I continued to teach and do all the things that a mother and wife need to do to survive. There were also times when I thought I could not go another day on the Journey I was walking. God held me close and he didn't let go even when I almost let go.

If you were wondering if there was a time I felt like taking my life I honestly have to say yes. There was a time when the cloud was not only over my head but also in front, back, all around and over my head. The only time I felt like taking my life one day was as I was driving over a place with guard rails. I thought to myself maybe it would be better if I did not have to go through this; if I just took the car and ran into the guard rail, the pain would end. I think that counts as a thought

> For anyone going through this kind of tragedy in their lives I advise the partner, parent or child of the ill patient to seek counseling separate for them. It is important to have someone to share everything including your fears as well as any other concerns you may have.

of taking my life. But, as I said before, God kept me and he didn't let go. I can't really say what my actual thoughts were about not going forward on the journey except to say I was tired. My love for Melissa and her welfare and my love for John and what would happen to him if I were not there for them helped me to change my mind.

Questions and Responses from John

Crisis Point Preface to Chapter 11
HOSPITALIZATIONS

Question 1: When did you first notice hearing voices inside your head?

John's Response: I didn't realize it until years after I was sick. I acted on things that came into my head. At Potomac Foundation in Maryland I felt that the voices were not mine. I couldn't trust them, but I knew I did not have to act on what they said. It took me a while because I still acted sometimes on what they said. For example: they told me to get up at 4 a.m. to go walking and I did.

Question 2: How early in your married life did you hear voices?

John's Response: I heard them in the very beginning of my married life when I look back and think about it. Some of the things I did I was not acting on my own. I would drink and drive and that was what was happening in my head not me.

Question 3: Had you ever experienced anything like this in your childhood and youth before you got married?

John's Response: I use to sit in the living room in the dark when I was growing up. As a teenager I use to run in the middle of the night for a long distance from my house and then run back. I said I was exercising. I think something was wrong. The voices bothered me for a long time; they just reared their head that night at IBM.

Question 4: How did you manage to cope with the job during this time?

John's Response: I did not cope well. I could not concentrate. The things I had learned looked new to me every day. They looked like things I had never done before.

Question 5: When did you actually leave your job, presumably for medical reasons?

John's Response: I left my job in 1983.

Question 6: How did you come to realize that these voices were not really you?

John's Response: I came to a point of no fear. I use to be fearful of the voices. They made my body feel like there was electricity all over me. I am not fearful of them anymore. I used to be afraid to go to sleep at night because the voices would cause me to wake up because they played games with my mind. When Barbara left I was alone and I had time to analyze my actions. I had no one to blame or to argue with. When I was at Taylor Manor I sometimes did what the voices told me to do.

Chapter 12

Hospitalizations

Once John was committed to the hospital he was taken to Saint Elizabeth's because that is where the ambulance transported him. I was later told that this was a stop only for evaluation. I wondered why they had not taken John to Montgomery General as before. When John called me from St. Elizabeth's he said to me "Why did you put me here, this is the worst place you could have ever put me. I am not like the people here." This was a bitter pill for me to swallow, because the ambulance driver told me that he was going to be taken to MG. The doctor at SE's had prepared to keep John there for treatment. I assured John I would get him out as soon as I could. I did what I said, but not without resistance from the hospital staff. SE's did not want to release him to Taylor Manor. I talked to one of the officials at SE and told them I was sending an ambulance for John and that I wanted him ready and if he was not I would sue the hospital. After a bit more conversation John was released picked up by ambulance and transported to TM.

John's stay at TM this time was about 2 months. When he came home it was evident to me that he was in better control of the illness. In time John became more and more fanatical about everything. He became obsessed with walking. He bought lots of sweats, gloves, hats and shoes for walking. He began race walking. He awoke at 2 or 3 o'clock in the morning, dressed and walked for an hour. The "voices" were more in control of his thoughts. John told me that he did not know the "voices" were controlling him. This was another scary time for Melissa and me. He returned to the house, played music, and stayed up the remainder of the day. John must have lost nearly 50 pounds.

John began to look sick due to the amount of weight he lost. People we knew began to ask if he were ill. He walked so much that he lost the first layer of skin from one of his feet. John pulled the skin off and continued walking. He cooked a lot in those days and the food was very healthy. As months became years John suffered more and more until he soon became so harsh with Melissa and me that things had to come to a head.

One Friday John was so harsh with Melissa that I made up my mind to leave the house and take Melissa with me. I told John that I was going to the hairdresser's, but really I was running away to a hotel until I could find a place for Melissa and me. When I left our home I had no intentions of ever returning until John got serious medical help. John looked for Melissa and me; he called the hairdresser to find out if we had been there. The hairdresser told him we had not been there. We left on Mother's Day weekend.

When John left home to attend church on Sunday Melissa and I came closer to our house. We went to a neighbor and wonderful friend where we could look at our house from her window. We slept there that night. Then we went to our house to wait for John. After waiting many hours John did not return. It just happened that his oldest brother came to the house that Sunday. I asked Edward to please drive me around so that we could find him. I looked everywhere, and then decided to call the police to ask if they had a report that might describe my husband. The police told me there was a report of a man walking down the middle of Veirs Mill Road. For anyone who does not know Viers Mill Road, it is one of the busiest roads in Wheaton. Somehow I knew in my heart that the man reported walking down the middle of Veirs Mill Road was John. The thought of my husband walking in the middle of Veirs Mill Road scared me to death.

During the time I was in the car with my brother-in-law I was thinking on more than one level. I was also in deep prayer the entire drive. I continued to repeat the 23rd Psalm over and over. I understood at that time the seriousness of writing God's words on the tablet of my heart. When we face a crisis and there is no Bible we must be prepared to remember God's words. I decided that Edward should drive to Wheaton Plaza. I thought that we might find John there. As Edward drove into Wheaton Plaza I spotted John's white station wagon. The car had been wrecked, but the keys were still in the ignition and the motor was still running. After turning the car off and taking the keys out of the ignition, I called a tow truck to have the car taken to the dealer. I began to share with the tow truck driver that I was looking for my husband and that I needed to get to the judge to have him committed to the hospital. At my request Edward was prepared to drive me to Rockville to petition the judge, but the tow truck driver told to me, no, go to the detention center because there was always a judge on duty. I did not hesitate to take his advice. I did not realize it at the time, but God had sent the tow truck driver to lead me to the next steps on the search for John so that I would be in the right spot at the right time.

Edward drove me to the detention center and as I sat there waiting for the judge the police came through the door with my husband, John, in handcuffs with his feet in whatever is used by the police to keep people from running away. I immediately rose to my feet and approached the police who said to me "sit down." My reply was no, I won't sit down because that is my husband and he is ill. I told the police that I was there to see the judge so that I could commit John to the hospital. The reply from the police was, "All right, we won't charge him because he is ill and you are here for him. He hit a police officer and was at a food store telling people not to shop at the store and throwing things all around. When we tried to subdue him he hit a police officer." The female officer said she knew John belonged to someone because he was clean and was wearing a suit. John told the officers that he was homeless. He was wearing the suit because he had done all of this after church. I was told by a member of the church that John had thrown away all of his personal belongings and anything that would identify him. This is the reason the police could not identify him.

The final words from the police officer were, "Lady, you can take him to any hospital you want, but only God can help this man." I asked the police to take John to a local hospital for examination and admittance until I could call Taylor Manor and have him committed there.

> It strikes me while writing that Edward never got up from his seat to approach John. He stood near his seat. I suppose He was afraid of what was happening to his brother. He had never been around when John was ill and having to be committed to the hospital.

As the police drove to the hospital I asked Edward to follow so that I could be at the hospital for his admittance. John knew I was there, but as with the first time he was admitted, the doctors thought that I caused him to become more agitated. I stayed as long as I could and then was taken home. Edward left shortly after we arrived home. He promised that he would return to check on John. He never returned nor did he call to ask about John. I felt sad that John was abandoned by his brother, but I was also angry that he never returned to check on him. That was the last time that John was committed to a mental institution.

I knew that God had saved him and I just needed to find him, wherever he was. I also knew that I was not going to find my husband by my understanding, but rather I would have to lean on the understanding of God because my understanding was inadequate. Was I scared, yes, it was one of those kinds of fears where you are frozen in time, but you react anyway. God gives us a well that we can tap into any time we need it. I tap into that well often. The well for me is a place where I can go to God in a way that I may not go every day.

Questions and Responses for John part of Chapter 11
HOSPITALIZATIONS

Question 1: Can you describe what it was like to be a patient in a psychiatric nursing home?

John's Response: I thought that the other people were crazy and I was sane. I recognized myself as having a problem. When I was at Montgomery General Hospital I had to go to group therapy meetings. One day someone asked me if I was an alcoholic. I answered no, I am not an alcoholic. After that day I never drank again. I thought I was normal. I did not understand where the voices were coming from. My problems were nothing like some of the other patients at Taylor Manor. At least that is what I thought.

Question 2: Did your illness worsen or subside at TM?

John's Response: The first time I was at TM I thought I had no problems. The second time I was at TM I participated in the things we did in shop. I liked making ceramic things. The third time I was there I realized I did have a problem. I got better after I recognized I had a problem. You have to recognize that you have a problem otherwise you see everyone as crazy and you are the only one sane.

Question 3: Describe having your wife and daughter come to visit you at Taylor Manor. What did you talk about? How did you feel?

John's Response: I felt isolated. I had nothing to say to Melissa, our daughter. I did not feel good when they left because I had to go back to the same old routine. I enjoyed the visits and I did not want them to end.

Question 4: Do you have any way of accounting for your change since Taylor Manor so that you and Barbara seem to be able to live rather peacefully together these days, despite your illness?

John's Response: The separation for me was the time I had to stand on my own two feet. I had no one to argue with. I also realized that no one could help me: I had to help myself. I did not have to be angry!

Chapter 13

Keeping Safe

When I left the house with Melissa this time it was as difficult as all other times. My heart ached for John and I had to be strong for Melissa who was now in the ninth grade. I spent the day before Easter looking for an apartment for Melissa and me. It was so sad and yet I knew for Melissa's survival I had to move and stay away. Actually, it was for John's and my survival as well. I remember going into one of the bedrooms of our house to pray each day that God would take this all away. Even after all the years of his illness I was still hopeful that the bitter cup of his illness would be removed. Melissa and I found two apartments. We decided to rent the apartment on Georgia Avenue that happened to be about 2 miles from our house.

After moving into the apartment I needed to get furniture, clothing, bedding and all the things needed to set up an apartment. I decided to go back to our home to gather items that Melissa and I needed to set up the apartment. Before Melissa and I came to the house I called the police to escort us to the house because I did not know how John would react. When we got to the house John would not allow us to enter the house. The police told him why we were there. His reply to the police was, "I don't know this person, I have never seen her before and no, she can't come into my house." When John opened the door and said that he did not know me or Melissa we were heartbroken. I felt that John was a person I did not know at this time. It appeared to me that he was laughing at me and saying to himself, I fixed you. I left without any items from the house. Lawfully, the police can't make him open the door for us to enter the house even when the house is in my name also. Walking away from the house was very painful.

Once John was at Taylor Manor this time, Melissa and I came to the house to get a bed, clothes, bedding and other things to set up our little apartment. I left the house and John with no intentions of returning. I felt at the time that nothing could be done to change the fear Melissa and I had experienced in the house. I felt that he did not want to change and I was tired and becoming physically ill from living with the stress of our lives over the years. The last visit I made to John at TM I tried to tell him that I would not be at the house when he returned: I don't think he understood that I was moving out of the house. I left a note in the house for John when Melissa and I left. She was so happy to leave the house, but I on the other hand felt a deep sense of grief. Grief and anger that John had suffered so long, that Melissa was happier away from the house where she had grown up, that I had grown tired and weary and no longer able to manage the illness, a job, being a mother and a caretaker. In all actuality I never did manage the illness.

In many ways I felt as if I had been a failure to John and Melissa. After all, I had been the person who always felt that I could take care of everything. I was strong and careful to manage our time and our lives together. I was the one who could stay in the triangle in the relationship between Melissa and her dad. Being in the triangle in this relationship was very difficult. There were times I wanted to run away or start to scream with pain and fear. Walking away from a home that we had made together was very emotional for me. After gathering all what we needed and that I could take in the car, I stopped at the front door, looked back and said a prayer for our family, closed the door and walked away in tears. Later, I asked a friend of Melissa's father to come to the house to get the bed and one of the arm chairs from the living room. There was no other way to do what I knew I had to do for Melissa and me. In many ways it was what I needed to do for the three of us.

Melissa and I set up the apartment and began our life away from John. She was so happy that we had left the house and her father. She could breath and she felt free to be a teenager without her father who kept an eye on her every move. She was free to be who she was and wear clothes she liked. She was so excited that we could go to the store to buy for her without her father's input. It appeared that she continued her life without a care for her dad. We went shopping and bought things that she liked to wear. I always took time to take her shopping and allowed her to have the freedom she so desperately needed.

Little did our precious daughter know that I was close to tears so many times when we were out shopping; I wanted to be fully present for her and at the same time I wanted to be where John was. I did not feel well because my heart was heavy and I was totally exhausted. I could have won an Oscar for the acting that I did for Melissa's sake.

After several months John arrived home to find he was alone in the house. He found the letter I had written on the little antique table in the living room. I had written to him and told him that I needed to leave him because there was no other way for me to help Melissa to mature. In the letter I told him that I needed to leave and that I needed to let God deal with him without me around.

Chapter 14

Living Apart

After returning home, John was here in the house alone for the six months. He knew where I worked and would call me at work. At first I did not speak to him, but found out quickly that he would not stop calling. Before leaving the house I had planted a garden of tomatoes and cucumbers. When they were ready John would come to my car, unlock the car and put the vegetables in the car. In the six months John and I never crossed each other's paths. I was, at that time, still very much afraid of John. I had not seen him since he returned from Taylor Manor and did not know that things were beginning to change gradually for him. God had begun to change our future the day I "ran" away. He knew the beginning and the ending as we were going through the valley.

I drove Melissa to work each day and shopped at the stores were John and I always shopped together. Throughout the entire 6 months John, Melissa and I never crossed paths. Melissa and I did not attend the church where we went as a family. We changed to another church. It is 19 years since I returned home. It was the last time John spent in a mental institution. John and I continue to be members of the church Melissa and I changed to. We never returned to the previous church.

It was painfully lonely in the apartment. Melissa was happy, but the longer I stayed away from John the more my heart crumbled. I was thankful that I had the counsel of my guardian angel, Sylvia. She always made me feel calm when she talked to me, but believe it or not, when I left her the feeling was short lived. I was alone and had to deal with my feelings. John visited Sylvia almost every day. She would tell me how he was acting and what he was saying to her. Early in the school year of 1991 I was alone in the apartment with such grief and sadness. At that moment I leaned against the wall and asked the Lord, "What is it that you want me to do?" At that very moment John called and asked me to come to have a soda with him. My answer was, yes, I will come. We met at what used to Bob's Big Boy on Georgia Avenue in Aspen Hill. We talked a lot and smiled a lot at each other. We said good-bye and that was the beginning of the second beginning in our lives as husband and wife.

John had changed so much from the way he was before I left. He was calmer and quite peaceful. He was not yelling or talking harshly; it was comfortable to be around him. John and I met many times after that. John took me to the movies and we ate out several times. John had been referred to a wonderful, special therapist by the name of Karen Blackburn. She was his psychiatric therapist. In mid October after John and I had discussed it for some time I decided that Melissa and I would return to our home. I left the house that had brought me so much pain and at that time I did not know that I could go back into the house that had so many skeletons that had haunted us for many days, months and years of fear.

Melissa and I came to the house to have dinner with John. I knew the moment I stepped back into the house that God had evicted all of the demons that I previously felt in the house. God had blessed the house from corner to corner. I felt at peace and safe in our home. John finally told me about Karen, his therapist. When John told Karen that we had been talking and "dating" she asked him if he would like to bring me to the sessions. John and I met with Karen together for the following 13 -14 years. Karen was the first therapist who recognized that John and I needed to work together as partners so that I would be able to call her if I saw something going wrong with John. John and I agreed that it would work and we would trust each other. John agreed that I should call Karen with any concerns I might have concerning his state of mind. When we told Karen my plan to return to the home after Halloween, which was about two weeks away, Karen asked the question "why are you waiting?" Her question caused us to think and we both responded, why not.

When I told Melissa that I made the decision to return to our home she asked, "Mom, why would you want to go back to him"? I told her that dad was a lot better and I felt safe with him. She did not want to come back to the house, but through it all she came back with me and began her life all over again. I think if she had had enough money and been older, she would have stayed in the apartment. I have never asked her if she regretted coming back home.

Melissa was born into a family that was ill. Long before she had any real idea what was happening in the family she was born into, she began processing in her own way what was happening. She could not understand all that she saw and heard and she had no control over what she did not understand. Early in the writing I wrote that Melissa had come through the many years of her father's illness well. On second thought, I don't believe that she made it through as well as I'd like to think she did. She found a way to cope and in doing so she held a lot inside that she did not understand.

Melissa's living with the fear, anger and apprehension of her sick family is enough to make me cry buckets of tears. I feel sad and a bit guilty that I could not protect her inside where she must have suffered many times. I could protect her as much as possible from the harshness of her father's voice, I was able to remove her from a situation that was causing her pain, but I could not protect her from that place that I could not see, her heart and her sinew. Guilt is a terrible thing so I will leave it behind now and continue to move on in the writing knowing that I did my best.

Would it have been better for Melissa to grow up without her father? I had the power to leave and to make a new life for her. I could have left him in an institution, divorced him and made a life for Melissa and me. As the years passed and we were suffering I never thought about leaving John in an institution. The following statements may sound strange, but somehow I knew in New York that I would have to go through many trials and tribulations with John. There were times that I thought of not having children because I was afraid of what life was going to bring in the years after we left New York. I always said to John that I never wanted to have children in New York, but in all honesty I was trying to stall having children all together.

I stated earlier that Melissa was all that I ever wanted in a child and she is and is still becoming the very special young woman I knew she would become. Melissa and I made it this far by the Grace of God. Melissa has observed me many years of her life in control of everything that needed to be taken care of. When she was old enough she observed me manage the fear, arrange hospital commitments for her dad, anger, and her father in the worst of times. What she did not see was the inside where I was suffering and literally falling apart. (Perhaps on a different level she too was broken.) She did not see the times that I wanted to cry or when her dad was at his worst, the grief I felt for him and for each of us in the family. I could not show the fear, anger, grief, and depression that I was going through because I had to be strong for her.

I thought that I had to let her see me strong and in control of all that was going on in our family. Sometimes I fooled myself into thinking I was in control, but as John became more ill, I knew that it was only by the grace of God that I was able to remain standing. There was no way for Melissa to understand the fear and sometimes, I admit, dread I felt when I had to return home to a very ill husband. Fear and dread because I never knew where John would be mentally and emotionally when I returned. It is possible that Melissa understood more than I think she did.

When I was a little girl I was so afraid of the night, not the dark so much as the night and what could be in the dark. I imagined there were things in the dark. I was not sure what was in the dark, but I felt that it was something there that could hurt me and if there was, I would have no control over what it would do to me. When John became so ill, I again became terrified of the darkness. In some ways John's illness frightened me so that I thought I had no control in the dark of the night. I stayed awake many nights without much sleep because I never knew whether I needed to escape from the house in the darkness and there would be no one to help Melissa and me. I planned in my mind how I would escape safely with Melissa when we had to escape.

In a situation such as Melissa and I lived it was imperative for me to plan for the unexpected. I planned a route of escape. We slept in our clothes for years. When we brought Melissa home I knew that I needed to keep her safe and ready at all times. Anyone in a situation like this, if possible plan to find a safe place for you to go in case of an emergency. If you have no friends and you are alone as we were, without family in the area, make sure that you have a credit card ready at all times to get to a hotel until you can make further plans.

John who is 6'4" inches could crush Melissa and me without thinking too hard. I knew this when he was ill, but it was not enough for me to know, I had to have a plan to get away. Survival or in control, I am not sure, but it made sense to me. I had to tell Melissa when she was old enough to understand during the deepest times of John's illness that there might be a time we would have to get out of the house fast and that if I said let's go, she was to move fast toward the front door and wait for me on the outside of the house. It actually happened one night that we did have to run. I mentioned this time earlier in the book; when I told Melissa that we had to go she did exactly what I told her. I shall never forget that as we drove away from the house Melissa looked back at the house and said to me "Momma, it is like the devil is laughing at us." I am not altogether sure I understood what these words meant to her, but I knew that she was so afraid and so aware that there was something terrible going on in our house.

Late in John's illness I learned that it was imperative for me to always have a bag packed for Melissa and for me with clothes for the season, toothbrushes, combs, and all that we would need until we could decide what to do. I made sure that we had enough medications for one week. I always told John that I needed to have a bag ready in case Melissa and I got stranded somewhere. He never questioned my reasoning for the bags. I also took blankets for Melissa and me in case we were caught on a night when it was cold. It was difficult, but necessary to lie to my husband. It was never comfortable to know that I had to be diligent and remember to change clothes for the season.

Once Melissa and I moved back to the home I never felt the need to keep clothes, medications and other necessities in the car. One might think that I would be careful not to trust that John would not become as ill as he was before we left the house and before his last hospital stay, but I know that through God's keeping He had prepared each of us to trust in Him only. I prayed that God would have His way and that He would take our will and make it His. Truthfully, I never gave it a thought that John would become so seriously ill again. We were fully under God's grace!

Chapter 15

Finding Peace Together

This section may appear to be out of place, but it is a return to our life after Melissa came back to the house. It was necessary to tell about Melissa and me and where I was because in many ways I feel that Melissa learned to be in control of everything she does by living with me during her father's illness.

After returning to the house we began our lives anew. We, as a family, composed an agreement of how we would respect each other. John was no longer fanatic about my coming and going; he treated Melissa with a lot of love and respect and he worked very hard to understand her needs as a teenager. When we returned to the house Melissa was going into tenth grade. John continued to be present for the important things in Melissa's education. One thing that John completely changed is the cooking, in fact, while writing this book I have just realized that he has, in many ways, taken off the old and put on the new. It is almost as if he can't cook. He has tried to tell me that he doesn't cook because it is my kitchen. I did complain a lot to Karen, our psychiatric nurse, about John's fanaticism about the cooking and menu planning. Today he is so very easy to please with the meals and the cooking. It is no longer necessary that I cook three meals each day and I never have to write out the menu for the week.

In some obscure sort of way we both learned to accept each other in a fresh new way. John never asks how long I am going to be gone when I go to meetings or if I have a staff meeting. I try to have a calendar on the refrigerator with all doctor's appointments and meetings after school. Learning to accept the change was a challenge for both of us. Accepting change in the cooking was more difficult for me because in some ways I liked the fact that John prepared the meals, but I had to accept that he was not about to do the same things in the kitchen that he did during the illness.

Moving back to the house was not in my plans and I never thought I could ever live in it again because of all the sadness and sickness, let alone the fear I had grown accustomed to. Actually, there was a possibility that we would not move back to this house, because John and I had decided to put the house up for sale. It was on the market for about two months and not a bite for purchase. Before leaving this house I felt there was something dark and ugly hanging over it and in every corner of each room. I suppose one could believe that I had learned to feel evil in the house and that would be a real, because I honestly felt that fear. When John called me that day when we were separated and my response to the invitation to meet him was yes, God was already working in the house to prepare it for our return. It is amazing to me as I write how God reveals to me how much He was with me all the way preparing a table for me. From the moment I walked back into our home I was sure that this was what God planned for us. I was not fearful of anything about the house because all of the fear was removed and replaced with love, peace and joy.

Don't think for a moment that there have not been some tense moments in the home, but John and I learned to respect each other even more than ever and John is able to talk with me about what the "voices" say and how they are bothering him during the day and how sometimes his sleep or as he says it "I am asleep and not asleep" or "they are playing games with me while I am asleep." Some days John gets up and goes downstairs to shave and when he comes back upstairs it is obvious to me that he has been and is still being disturbed while in his bathroom downstairs. It is obvious because of his walk and his disturbed expression. When I ask him how he is feeling, his reply is always "I'm okay." It is sad to me that John never says that he feels great today and not even that he feels good. I used to want to hear that he felt great, but I accept the fact that I am not the one who is experiencing the "voices" in my head. Some mornings John tells me that the "voices" have been bothering him since he got up. Almost every Sunday morning when he is preparing to go get ready for church the voices become more disturbing to John. He tells me that the "voices" are making his mouth move to say curse words that he is not saying. When he tells me this he is always disturbed because he feels that he can't control his mouth, but it is the "voices" that are controlling his mouth. You wonder what I say when John tells me this? No, I am not afraid though there was a time that my heart would start to pump and my mind would begin to race with fear and dread at what he said. I have learned to listen and to listen with careful ears to whether John is in control of what he has said.

I know that he is still in control when he is able to continue to get ready for church or to continue doing what he is doing. After he tells me how he feels or that the "voices" are causing his lips to move, he seems a bit relieved. I am also relieved that I am able to listen and hear without having to try to make him feel better or that everything will be fine. I have also noticed that once it is said, John and I can talk a little about the "voices" and then move on. He is more in control and able to ignore the voices. So he moves on with his preparations for church.

John and I spend a lot of time together. There is hardly a day that I come home that he is not here waiting for me. He takes care of the family finances, he washes and folds and is helpful to me in many ways. No, he does not cook very much, but when he does, I am so grateful. He can make delicious popcorn, but always tells me that I make the best popcorn so that he does not have to make it, I know that! This tickles me because he just wants me to make it because it tastes better when someone else makes it. Every once in a while, maybe once or twice a year, John has a doctor's appointment at 3 p.m. that lasts until after I am home from work. Once I come into the house it takes me at least 10 to 15 minutes to realize that I am in the house all alone and the house belongs to me and only me. By the time I get a bit used to it, John is returning and I am at the door to greet him and welcome him home.

One might wonder how I can do this day after day and year after year. It is not difficult, but I will admit it is great to have the time alone once in a while. John and I respect each other's time alone. I can be in the bedroom and he in the sitting room and it is as if we are alone. We can be alone like this for hours and feel fine about the aloneness in the same house. I have found that I use my evening to be alone to read, do Bible study, to talk on the phone or to work on a project. I also stay up sometimes after John is in bed just to have time alone in the same room.

Eighteen years ago we were separated, but today I would not give anything for the life we have as a family. Melissa and her father are close in a way that I am unable to touch. They have disagreements; they say what they need to say to each other, then they move on. Melissa gets angry with her dad because he reminds her of something she needs to think about, but she never leaves our home angry. Melissa has a chronic illness and sometimes she must stay with us for several days. I am happy to say that she stays with us a lot less frequently than a year ago. Her father goes into the kitchen to cook for her whether he knows how to or not. They engage in a serious conversation sometimes when she visits. I am often in another room when they talk, but I can often hear pieces of their conversation and I just smile with a joy that cannot be explained in words. When John was very ill he was grouchy and fussy and many times their conversations were fraught with anger that was never settled.

John would, as I, feel blessed to see Melissa married to a very special man to share her life. There is, too, the fact that I have hovered over Melissa and to this day I have tried to protect her from all that could harm her. For the past two to three years it has been my goal to leave her room to grow in her own way. It is difficult beyond all that one can imagine for me to decide to step back. Not only is it difficult to allow her to experience the hurt and disappointment that will come into her life, but it is also difficult because she is an only child

Sometimes it is a struggle for the two of us because Melissa is independent, hardheaded and stubborn at times. These facts make it more difficult to move out of her way and let her feel life her way, but I am trying with all of my might for her and for myself. If I try to deal with her life I am unable to deal with my own. I must constantly remind myself that I am not the fixer of every situation she is having. When Melissa was a baby and later a young child I had to take care because of the situation we were in. I have learned that I don't always have to be giving. With the help of God I will continue to grow stronger and continue to not allow myself to feel so deeply as it pertains to her life. All that I have said about how I am learning to give Melissa space to grow sounds easy, but is not the least bit easy any day of the week.

I wrote earlier that once Melissa went to college she has not lived with us for any length of time. She moved to an apartment with two of her friends and then to her own home. John and I continue to grow closer as the years go by. We have had a lot of renovations to our home. John was home while I worked; he was busy getting estimates for the work that was to be done on the house. He was also here in the house so that workers could come to the house and remain for the day. John is very good when it comes to overseeing the work that has to be done by a contractor. If you think that he has done this without the "voices" you are wrong. Each and every day "they" are present and attempting to influence his decisions and thoughts.

In some ways John and I have become even closer than we were before I left our home. We have always worked well together, so much so that sometimes we are thinking the same thoughts at any given time. The following are a few examples of this. Today we were riding in the car to take care of an errand. Most of the trip we were both in deep reflection and thought. I was thinking to myself, we are in Rockville so we should stop by the showroom to get the new toilet seats that we needed. I never voiced what I was thinking, but as we began to get closer to the showroom John said "the toilet seats" and nothing more. My reply was, yes, I was thinking the same thing. Earlier the same day John had ridden with me to take my car for service and when the service technician came to explain something else that needed to be done to the car I looked across the room as John looked me in the eyes and nodded, yes, for my approval. I nodded back without hesitation because I respect what he determines is appropriate for the car.

We are planning to purchase a new computer soon; the day after Thanksgiving there was a great price on the very computer we wanted. John decided last night that we should purchase the computer, but after much thought I told him that I thought we should wait a bit longer. He asked me several times today if I still felt that we should wait. My reply was, yes, we should wait. He respected my decision. We did not get the computer.

Sharing these incidents with you creates a clearer picture of the man who hears "voices" and who must always keep his guard up. I often think to myself how difficult that must be for him. I find myself in reflective thought a lot during the course of a day and my thoughts are not invaded by "something" that talks to me as with situations with John. It is truly impossible for me to even imagine fully what is happening in his head and that his thoughts are not really his.

I have not walked in his shoes and have often heard John say that he would not wish what is happening to him on anyone. God is so merciful, because as I prayed some thirty years ago for a complete healing, He made it possible for John to live life in spite of his disability. God has taught him to be caring, loving and generous. He gave him the ability to take care of the finances in the family and to make important decisions for our family.

As you have read, you realize that God's time for the miracle was not my time. I wanted the healing right away. I wanted to stop mourning for my sick husband, to feel safe in my home, to make it safe for Melissa to grow up healthy and happy and for John to see that the thoughts were his and not what he called "voices." It took many years of being in the valley and going through the storm before I realized God was working on His time for our family. It was so easy to tell God how to make it better, but He truly began to answer my prayers when I had no more advice and I realized that He could make the miracle without my help.

Sometimes I feel discouraged but not defeated by the negative thoughts that come into my head about the writing. The writing has been a struggle for me in many ways. I continue because of the support of friends and family and because someone needs to hear this story.

I am going to be obedient until the end no matter how difficult it becomes. The most negative thoughts I have had recently are concerning John. The negative, discouraging thought is that John will be hurt by this story. I know in my heart that God will take care of this, but the thought continues to surface. I feel it necessary to share that with readers who might think that I have found this easy to write. I also need to say that I am not writing of my own free will; it is God who leads me in my thoughts. After all, He did promise that He would show me how to tell the story.

I know there are negative forces in the world that come to steal and to defeat. I must know always that my guide is God and even as I express to you what I am feeling, I know that God is in control and He will continue to give me clarity of mind to complete my story so that it will help someone who needs to hear from John, Melissa and me.

January 8, 2008

Even as I write today there is an incident I want to share with you, the reader, about John and how things were for him for several days. I noticed that he was snappy and grouchy on Saturday, Sunday and Monday. I was not sure what was going on so I observed and listened in order to understand. On Monday I said to John, let's go out to have lemonade and then go to the grocery store to pick up a few things. When he came out of the house I immediately sensed that he was tense and uptight. As I drove we began to talk about the our day and John shared with me that the "voices" had been extremely active during the day so much so that he almost fell when he stepped down from the office where the money for gas is collected. He confided in me that "they" had been very active since Saturday. I asked if he knew why the "voices" were so active right now. He shared he wanted to lose weight, but the "voices" were working on him overtime trying to discourage him. Discouragements by the "voices" is nothing new for John, but remember, as was shared earlier, John has "voices" that are negative and want him to fail. After our sharing I hear a sigh from John and I sensed that he was not as uptight any longer. By Tuesday John had his defenses up and was in a better mood because he was fully aware of what was happening and how to manage it. You might think that he should be ready and already prepared when he is going to try something new, but when there is something always chattering in your head you probably need to rest the mind sometime.

I share this incident with the reader with the intention of giving the reader a clearer picture of how I have learned over many years to be quiet, respectful, observant, and unafraid to talk with John about what is going on. It took many years for me to learn to wait and be unafraid. I did not learn this on my own: I had to pray and depend on God to bless me and help me to learn to be unafraid and brave enough to open the conversation with John. To tell John he will be all right is not enough; I must be brave and trust that God is always present and I need only to look to Him because He will carry me through the times when I may fear what John needs to say.

I admit that it is not always easy for me, but I know that I am never alone and I also know that I am able to tell if John is in trouble with the "voices" and whether he can manage the situation. If I close up and become fearful I could miss helping him and in turn help myself. I not angry about the fact that I must always be alert, I am no longer angry about the illness or John's state of mind. As I shared earlier in the book, when a family member is ill, each family member takes on new roles.

This tragedy caused stress, sadness and anger. Sadness because John will always need to be on a variety of medications, he will not be able to have a career, and he will forever need be on guard. Stress because sometimes it is difficult to be the main breadwinner in the family and I don't always find it easy to relax. Anger because we never invited this illness to invade our lives and once it did there was little we could do about it. Though I have all of these feelings I am sustained in the words of the 23rd Psalm. "The Lord is my Shepherd and I can be confident that as I walk through every valley He will protect me and keep me." He always "leads me beside the still waters." God allows me to stand still until His will is clear to me. The only way I can stand is through the love of God. When he is with me there is no reason to be fearful.

For over 35 years John and I have tried to walk with God. We have prayed together, we have trusted His word and we have depended on Him completely. In anything that we have faced, we have called on God for guidance and He has given us safe harbor. Sometimes the ships we've sailed on have gone all the way into the storms where we had to stand still and know that He is God and we are His children. We have remembered that Jesus loves us because the Bible tells us so. The depth of our love for God is so great, but we also know that He first loved us.

Even when you don't know how you are going to make it in life and no matter what may come at you in your marriage, you can depend on a Savior, the same Savior John and I continue to depend on.

Final Interview Questions from John

Question: If a spouse of someone diagnosed with schizophrenia came to you for advice, what would you say?

John's Response: In the workplace I would advise the spouse to confide in the doctors at work. When things get unbearable at work have a conversation with the manager and perhaps take some time off work.

Regarding Religion: Rely on your religion very heavily. Religion is the only thing that saved me. I read the Bible every day even though I did not understand everything. I tried to think of how the words in the Bible applied to me. You have to be careful not to become fanatical about the Bible. Sometimes you can tend to think that it is God speaking to you and it really is the voices telling you to act on something that is wrong.

Regarding Prayer: Pray a lot. Be careful not to become over religious. Try to distinguish what is entering your head and if is good thinking. Church could actually push you over the edge if you don't question some of the things you hear. Analyze and apply to you and what your needs are in your life.

Regarding Faith: At one point during the illness, I thought I had no faith. I thought the pain of the illness would never go away. I thought things would never change for me. It was unbearable. I could not see the light at the end of the tunnel. I could not look ahead. When I began to accept that the voices were going to be with me and that I did have a problem I slowly regained my faith.

Note: I would also tell the spouse that the voices should be recognized as not your voice. They are independent of you. Don't act on anything they say especially if it is harmful to you or someone else. Knowing that the voices are separate is the only way to survive. Even when you recognize them as separate they can control your mind. It is like mind control which I never believed in.

Doctor: The spouse should seek out a good doctor. The spouse should always stay on the medication it is the only way to function. When you are off the medication the voices can influence you and take over.

Epilogue: Continued Journey

Writing our family story, our journey in the world of schizophrenia has not been easy. As I have come to the end of the writing, but the journey continues for John, Melissa and me. This is a journey that never ends. It continues because the medical community to date has not discovered any drug or treatment that ends the nightmare for all who live in this world. What we hope for the reader is that we have presented our story with suggestions and revealing eye openers that have made or will make a difference in the manner in which you view schizophrenia and other mental illnesses.

John and I continue to grow in faith with constant attention to what is a part of our lives. We both have grown as this true story unfolded. Together we have faced very scary moments in our lives. As we shared during the writing and the process of the interview we told each other parts of our lives that one of us may not have remembered while going through. In many instances John was more specific about what happened at a given time in the depths of the illness while at other times he did not remember parts of our lives that I remembered vividly. We have become stronger by writing and sharing our story.

Last Thursday, June 12, 2009 I asked our daughter Melissa if she would ever read the book. I am encouraged by her response, "maybe.". Her voice offered hope that she too, would soon be ready to begin to remember so that she can continue to heal and grow. John and I reconnected with our therapist Karen Blackburn recently. We shared what our lives have been like since she retired and moved to another state. I shared with Karen that Melissa was not ready to remember the journey. Karen's response was, "yes, it would be good for her to remember, but she is afraid." My purpose for sharing this is to let the reader know how much I respect Karen and what she has to say. Her gentle words meant as much today as they did when we were under her care. It is not that I hadn't thought that Melissa was afraid, but more that Karen's validation of what I felt was soothing even when shared in an email.

There is always hope! The message of hope is powerful for anyone who may face schizophrenia with a loved one. Always believing that situations can change and to believe it with all of your heart even when you can no longer see hope, continue to **hope**!

It is extremely difficult to **believe** and remain hopeful even when all around you see nothing but disaster, but continue to believe that change will happen and do all that you can to make change come sooner rather than later. Dark days can and will surely visit your life, there will be hills to climb, valleys to conquer and at the end of the severe storms of schizophrenia there is **light**. Some days it will appear that a cloud has been cast over your life and there is something evil making fun of all of your attempts to believe but, continue to **believe**! In the darkest moments of your journey in the world of this insidious illness you will be left exhausted, confused and sometimes feeling extremely helpless, continue to believe!

My prayer for anyone reading this book is that you will become more sensitive and understanding of those who suffer with a mental illness. As a society we have made advancements in many areas of life, but there has not been much change in the mind of some who continue to cast a stigma on any individuals who does not see the world the way they may see it. Of course, we cannot truly see through the eyes of an individual suffering with a mental illness, but please, I beg you, try to be empathetic and as understanding as possible.

Remember that no one asks for a mental illness. Mental illness just invades the life of individuals without their permission and takes up residence for a lifetime. Mental illness can invade at any given time and will not ask whether the age or date is good. Mental illness strikes across color lines, race, gender and age.

In the writing of the book I shared with the reader that I morn what John' life might have been had he lived a life free of the illness of schizophrenia. I no longer morn because I have moved on to help make our life together as beautiful as it is today.

My life would have been different had we not had the illness to strike our family and take us on an unexpected journey. I would not change what I have gone through with my dear husband, John. I have grown in all areas of my life. I don't know what life would have been without John, but I admit without pain and all honesty that I have lived the life that was planned for me and I accept it all and I Count it all Joy. (James 1:2)

Thank you for reading our story and may you be as blessed as we are. Perhaps you, like I will pray for a healing and your prayer, like mine, will not be answered the way you want it, but be assured that whatever happens is best for you if you trust with all of your heart and believe that you are never alone. You are never alone.

Appendix

The following poem was written by Melissa at the age of 17. The poem is a reflection of what Melissa experienced during some difficult times in her life during the darkest days of her father's illness.

The Forgotten Exodus
Years ago and actions past, she remembers...
Now an Old woman, now Young again.
Closing her eyes, she breathes in Now and breathes out
Then.
She rocks ... and tries to remember ...

Moments ago a girl, bittersweet memories flood her...
A night Remembered, a night of chance.
Closing her eyes, she sees the scenes through dark clouds of
Time.
She rocks ... and tries to remember ...

An exodus in the night, fleeing some unseen ghost ...
Her mother Crying, her mother now Strong.
Closing her eyes, she hears distorted mother's pleas and
Warnings.
She rocks ... and tries to remember ....

A frenzy of coats tossed over comforting nightgowns …
Lives once Still, Lives now Running.
Closing her eyes, she feels the pointed ground under her
Barefeet.
She rocks … and tries to remember ….

A road ahead, uncertain and twisted, lays silently …
Tears wet creases of Smiles, Tears wet thoughts of Tomorrow.
Closing her eyes, she sees the Turn through naked trees'
Arms.
She rocks … and tries to remember ….

Years ago and actions past, she remembers …
Now an Old woman, Now Young again.
Closing her eyes, she breathes in Now and breathes out
Then.
She rocks and desperately tries to forget.
    © 2010   MC

The following two pages John and I share one of many of our separate prayers. John granted permission for me to share the following prayer which was written May 26, 1991 when we were apart from one another and he was still at Taylor Manor. I read his prayers for the first time several weeks ago. John's prayers are pure and while reading many of them I was brought to tears. I take the liberty to name this prayer "A Letter to the Father."

A Letter to the Father (May 26, 1991)
Before Leaving Taylor Manor Hospital
By John R. Covington

Dear Lord,

My day thus far has been a restful one. I have been thinking about my family once again. I miss them so much. I again have hoped they would have come up to visit me. But this was to no avail. I am forever circumspect of my life. Was I such a mean husband and father? I can't hear from my wife or daughter. Please watch over them Father. Please let them know that I miss them very much. Tomorrow is Memorial Day-I hope with your help that I get through tomorrow. I look forward to leaving here on Tuesday. But, of course, I shall feel very much alone when I get home. I know you will be there-just as you have always been. Please bring my family back to me. I love you and praise you father. Help me with my coming weeks alone. This I pray.

Amen

Private Moments with God
written April 4, 1991(Before leaving our home and before John was
admitted to Taylor Manor Hospital)
By Barbara Covington

Lord, I have felt and seen these hard times coming for John. Not certain why, but the feeling is real. I've said each day now for what seems more than a week- he will get along in the illness and without my help. I am here for him, but I can't and won't allow myself to go to that place. You know all about me Lord and in knowing you know that I am not totally without feelings, but thanks be to you I am not afraid. That old silly scary feeling wants to creep in, but I am trusting in you Lord and I know that in you there is no fear. I am at work today very early as you know because John and I are sharing one car. It is quiet and peaceful and the quietness affords me time to write to you now. Now, Lord as I end this time I end with thanksgiving for your blessings and a prayer for John.

In the Midst

John, as you struggle today with the unknown, remember the day you took the Lord into your life. He surrounded you with his angels and gave you a new life and freedom. I pray that you, Lord will lift the veil for John. If you will give him sunshine – not rain-light not darkness and Lord remind him that he can continue each day to surrender all to you. These and all other blessings I pray in the name of Jesus, your Son.

Amen and Amen.

Thank you, Lord.

This letter was written by Melissa after I asked her permission to include some of her story in the book.

Thursday, September 27, 2007

Mom,
I knew what it must be about. You have my blessing. I hope this is a blessing for you, Dad, me and my family as well. Don't be afraid to write as deep as you need. I learned more than even I knew...It flows well. I know it will be a blessing for others as well.

God bless you as you make this journey. I know it will not be an easy one.

Thank you for sharing it with me.

Love you,
Library Baby

www.ingramcontent.com/pod-product-compliance
Lightning Source LLC
Chambersburg PA
CBHW030347290526
45785CB00004B/1631